WINNING WORLD WAR II

A COMPLETE
ILLUSTRATED HISTORY

DAVID SCHONAUER

CENTENNIAL BOOKS

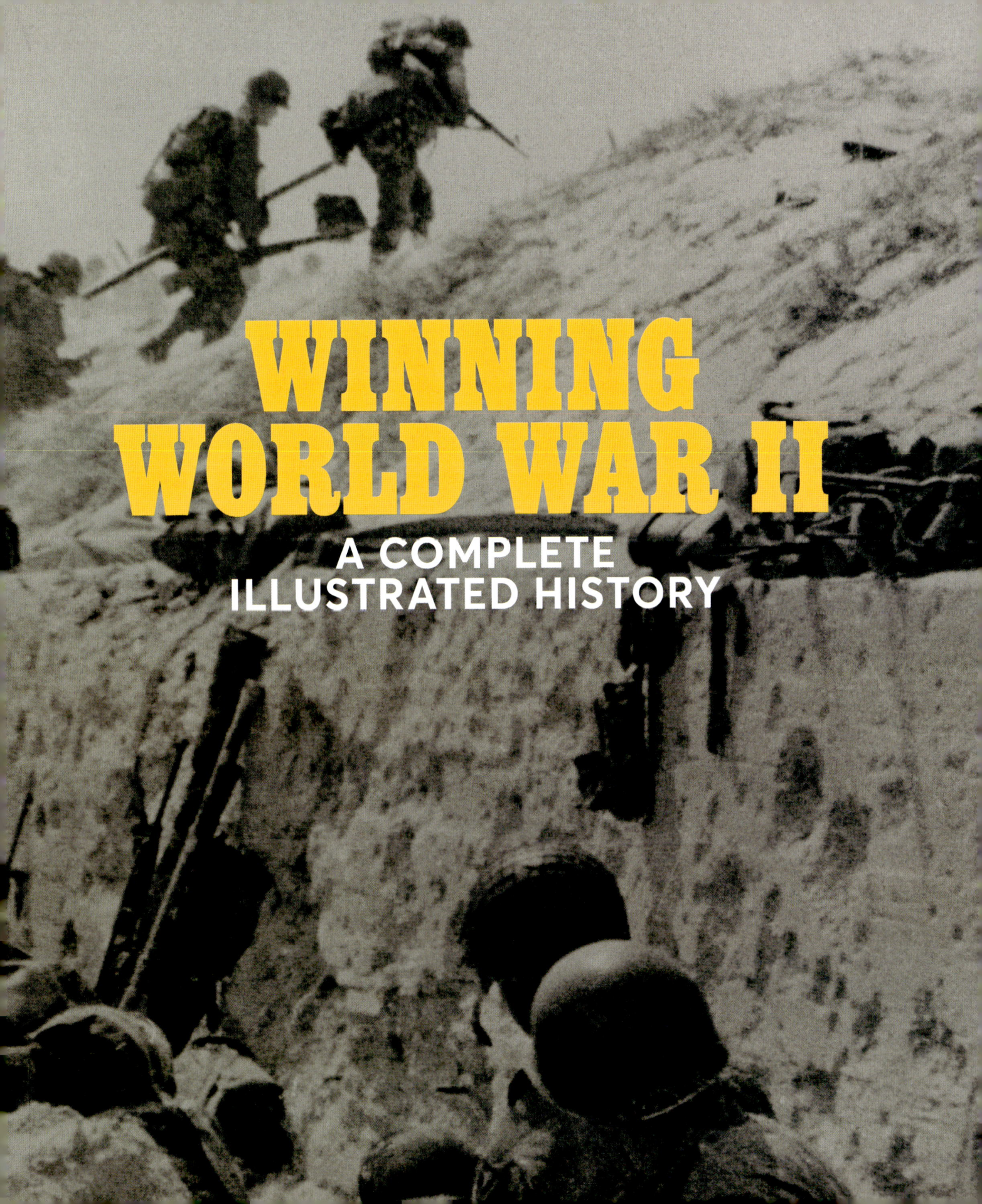

WINNING WORLD WAR II

A COMPLETE ILLUSTRATED HISTORY

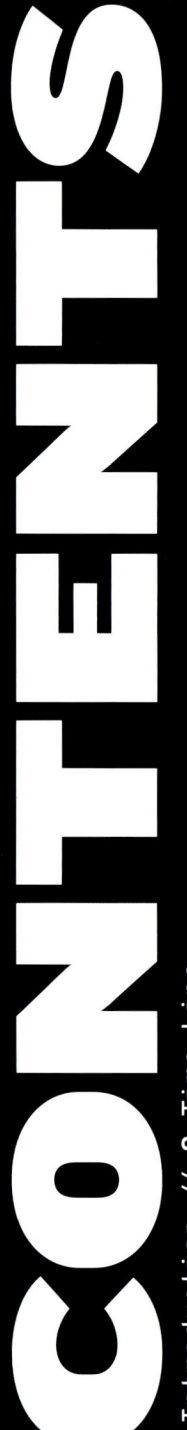

CONTENTS

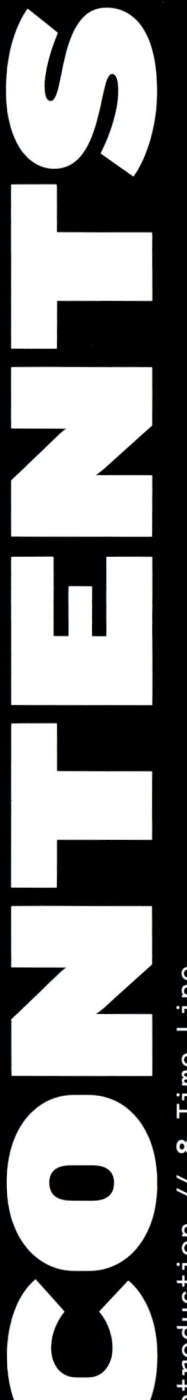

82

158

WAR AND REMEMBRANCE

THE WORLD WOULD BE A VERY DIFFERENT PLACE IF THE ALLIES HAD NOT BEEN VICTORIOUS IN THEIR FIGHT.

IT HAPPENED EARLY on the morning of Sunday, Sept. 2, 1945, in Tokyo Bay, on the 45,000-ton battleship USS *Missouri*, the flagship of the U.S. Navy's Third Fleet. Black-and-white newsreel films captured the moment as United States Army five-star Gen. Douglas MacArthur, the supreme allied commander for the occupation of postwar Japan, boarded the ship to accept the final capitulation of the Empire of Japan.

It was on another Sunday morning a little more than three and a half years earlier that the U.S. had gone to war, after Japanese aircraft attacked the Pearl Harbor naval base in Hawaii on Dec. 7, 1941—which President Franklin D. Roosevelt called a "date which will live in infamy." In the following weeks, Japanese forces unleashed an assault over a vast front in the Pacific, sweeping aside feeble resistance from Great Britain and the United States.

In March 1942, Gen. MacArthur, as commander of U.S. Army Forces in the Far East, had been driven

from the Philippines, vowing as he fled, "I shall return." He had then helped lead an astonishing effort to do just that, and in October of 1944 he waded ashore on the Philippine island of Leyte. The scene was immortalized by a *Life* magazine photographer named Carl Mydans, who had his own history with the Philippines and the Japanese.

In 1942, Mydans and his wife, Shelley, a *Life* reporter, had been stationed in Manila and were taken prisoner when the city fell into the control of the Japanese forces. They spent almost two years in captivity before finally being released in a prisoner exchange. Mydans was sent to cover the war's European Theater, where Allied armies were turning the tide in the struggle to defeat Nazi Germany. But he eventually found his way back to the fighting in the Pacific.

He returned to the Philippines with MacArthur, and he was with him that day on the USS *Missouri* when the war came to a ceremonial end. Years later, he recalled the solemnity of the occasion as

Japanese Foreign Minister Mamoru Shigemitsu walked toward a table to sign the formal instrument of surrender. Shigemitsu had been injured in an incident before the war, and Mydans remembered "the woeful sound" of his artificial

Photographer Carl Mydans documented the formal surrender of Japan aboard the USS *Missouri*.

leg "tapping out his progress to surrender his country."

"As he approached, my vindictiveness began to disappear and compassion replaced it," Mydans said. It was, he added, a "heartbreaking scene."

The following pages tell the story of a war that took place more than 75 years ago, but the lessons to be drawn are as starkly significant now as they were then. The legacy of WWII teaches us how societies steeped in seething hatred and

unchecked nationalism once set out on disastrous paths that led the world into an abyss of bloodshed. We must never forget what happened then, nor how out of that ferocity a new world emerged offering the promises of peace.
—*David Schonauer*

ROAD TO
CATACLYSM

HOW THE WORLD FOUND ITSELF ON THE BRINK OF
DESTRUCTION IN ALL CORNERS OF THE GLOBE.

The attack on
Pearl Harbor
thrusts the
U.S. into war.

JAPS BOMB HAWAII
DECLARE WAR ON U.S. AND BRITAIN

Hitler's
first radio
broadcast as
chancellor.

1940

MAY 10 Nazis
launch
blitzkrieg;
in six weeks
they conquer
Belgium, the
Netherlands,
Luxembourg and
France.

MAY 26 British
forces,
cornered by
German forces
on the French
coast, begins
evacuation
at Dunkirk.

AUG. 12 The
Luftwaffe
begin assault
on British
airfields,
kicking off
the Battle of
Britain.

SEPT. 27
Germany, Italy
and Japan sign
the Tripartite
Pact, creating
the Axis Powers.

1941

JUNE 22 Hitler
launches
Operation
Barbarossa,
sending
3 million
troops to
invade Russia.

DEC. 7 The
Japanese attack
Pearl Harbor.
On Dec. 8, the
U.S. declares
war against
Japan. On
Dec. 11, Italy
and Germany
declare war
against the U.S.

1939

SEPT. 1 Germany
launches
a surprise
invasion of
Poland,
launching war
in Europe.

SEPT. 3
Honoring their
treaty with
Poland, France
and Great
Britain enter
the war against
Germany.

1938

MARCH 12
Hitler annexes
Austria.
On Sept. 28, the
Munich Pact is
signed, which
allows Hitler
to annex the
Sudetenland
from
Czechoslovakia.

1933

JAN. 30
Adolf Hitler
becomes
chancellor
of Germany.

1937

JULY 7
Japan invades
China.

German soldiers
invade Poland.

U.S. forces battle in the Coral Sea.

The second bomb drops on Japan.

1945

FEB. 19 Marines land on Iwo Jima. The intense fighting lasts a month, and 6,821 Americans die.

APRIL 1 The battle to take Okinawa commences. By June 22, 92,000 Japanese soldiers and as many as 100,000 Okinawan civilians are dead. The United States suffers 12,000 military deaths and 60,000 wounded—the worst U.S. losses during the war in the Pacific.

APRIL 12 President Franklin D. Roosevelt dies. Harry S. Truman is sworn in as the 33rd president of the United States. On April 16, the Russians begin a massive assault on Berlin.

APRIL 30 Adolf Hitler dies by suicide in his Berlin bunker.

MAY 7 Germany surrenders.

JULY 16 The United States successfully tests an atomic bomb in New Mexico.

AUG. 6 A U.S. bomber drops an atomic bomb on the Japanese city of Hiroshima. On Aug. 9, a second atomic bomb is dropped on the city of Nagasaki.

AUG. 14 Japan accepts terms for unconditional surrender, ending the war.

1944

JUNE 5 Rome falls to the Allies.

JUNE 6 D–Day begins as the Allies invade Normandy.

JUNE 15 The Battle of Saipan in the Pacific begins. In three weeks of fighting, U.S. forces suffer 3,000 dead and 13,000 wounded. The Japanese lose some 27,000 soldiers.

JULY 20 A German cabal fails to assassinate Adolf Hitler.

AUG. 25 The Allies liberate Paris from German control.

DEC. 16 The Germans launch a last-ditch counterattack in the Battle of the Bulge.

1942

JAN. 20 The Wannsee Conference in Germany establishes the "Final Solution" for Jews in Europe. The Nazi plan would attempt to exterminate an estimated 11 million people.

APRIL 18 Sixteen B-25 aircraft carrier-launched bombers, led by Lt. Col. James Doolittle, strike Tokyo.

MAY 4–8 The Battle of the Coral Sea is the first battle between aircraft carriers.

JUNE 4 The Battle of Midway begins in the Pacific. It ends on June 7 with an American victory.

AUG. 7 U.S. land forces go on the offensive for the first time in the Pacific, touching down on Guadalcanal.

AUG. 23 The Battle of Stalingrad begins. It will end in a momentous Nazi defeat the following February.

NOV. 8 Operation Torch opens as Allied forces land in North Africa.

1943

JULY 10 Allied forces land in Sicily and gain control of the Mediterranean. In September, Allies land in Italy.

SEPT. 8 Italy accepts Allied surrender terms. German troops move to take control of the country.

NOV. 20 The Battle of Tarawa begins in the Pacific. U.S. Marines win a victory, but at the cost of some 1,000 American lives.

Allied troops storm the beaches at Normandy.

CHAPTER 1

THE GATHERING STORM

LOOKING FOR A PATH TO THE FUTURE,
THE GREAT NATIONS OF THE WORLD INSTEAD FOUND
THE ROAD TO WAR. THIS IS HOW IT HAPPENED.

Adolf Hitler leaves Bavaria's Landsberg Prison in 1924.

DESCENT INTO DARKNESS

AFTER WORLD WAR I, A FRACTURED EUROPE
SEETHED WITH FRUSTRATION AND RACIAL
HATRED, WHILE RISING MILITARISM
IN JAPAN FUELED DREAMS OF CONQUEST.
THE STAGE WAS SET FOR DISASTER.

THERE WAS TROUBLE in the air on Jan. 30, 1933. America's newspapers featured reports from Europe that day that were filled with a sense of deep apprehension.

"Adolph Hitler rose to power in Germany today on the rising tide of his militant Fascism," noted *The Cleveland Press*, which managed to misspell the first name of the new German leader.

There was foreboding in the analysis from Philadelphia's *Evening Bulletin*: "Adolf Hitler today was named Chancellor of Germany and the Republic has entered upon an adventure whose ending cannot be foreseen," read its story.

The New York Times provided some hope for readers worried about Europe's future: "Hitler Made Chancellor of Germany But Coalition Cabinet Limits Power," was its front-page headline.

The *Philadelphia Bulletin* also noted that Hitler, the 43-year-old leader of the National Socialist German Workers Party—the Nazis—did not yet have absolute political control over his country. The president of the German Republic, Paul von Hindenburg, a venerable statesman who had led the German army in World War I, had no intention of letting Hitler install a fascist government or a permanent dictatorship, if it could be prevented, the newspaper assured its readers.

"The question is," the *Bulletin* added, "can it be prevented?"

THE RISE OF HATE

If there was disquiet in the reports, there was also bewilderment: How did it happen? How did an "insignificant little man with a

Charlie Chaplin mustache" (as Hitler was described in the *Evening Bulletin* story) come to power?

Historians have been trying to answer those questions ever since. Among the best-known studies of Hitler's Germany is William L. Shirer's *The Rise and Fall of the Third Reich*, which was published in 1960, just 15 years after the end of World War II. Shirer, a young American journalist stationed in Berlin in the 1930s, had a firsthand view of what happened in Germany—"this great but baffling nation," as he called it. In 1,250

pages, he depicted a country in the thrall of an all-consuming hatred.

That hate grew out of deep wounds left by Germany's defeat in World War I. The Versailles Treaty, which ended that conflict, imposed harsh peace terms on Germany, including the loss of territory and costly war reparations. The Weimar Republic, the name given to the German state in the 1920s, printed money to pay the victors, resulting in hyperinflation: A loaf of bread in Berlin that cost 200 marks early in 1923 cost 200,000,000,000 marks by November. Berlin's cabarets were

Hitler sits in prison after being convicted of treason following the Beer Hall Putsch of 1923.

Hitler foresaw opportunity in the festering resentment gripping Germany in the 1920s.

Benito Mussolini
(center) and his
Fascist Party rose to
power in Italy in 1922.

filled with merrymakers intent on spending money at night, knowing it might be worthless by morning.

By the mid-1920s, Germany's economy had stabilized, but the Wall Street crash of 1929 sent it into a tailspin once more. And with economic hardship and festering resentment came growing social unrest. Violent paramilitary groups backing both the far left and far right flourished in the tumult.

FROM FAILED PUTSCH TO POWER

Hitler found his life's meaning in the growing economic and social chaos. Born in Austria and drawn to German nationalist sentiment from an early age, he'd served in the German army in the Great War and been wounded. After the war he perched himself in Munich and became involved in the roiling politics of the Nazi Party, which advocated belligerent nationalism and virulent anti-Semitism.

His role in the notorious Beer Hall Putsch in 1923—a comically unsuccessful Nazi coup d'état of the Bavarian government—landed Hitler in prison for nine months. There he began writing an autobiography called *Mein Kampf* ("My Struggle"), in which he lamented the woes besetting Germany, including its need for "Lebensraum," or "living space," and the "mongrel races" sapping its strength. After his release, Hitler organized the Nazis into a potent political and propaganda machine, abetted by the Sturmabteilung, or SA, a thuggish paramilitary group also known as the Brownshirts, who were used to intimidate political opponents and Germany's Jews.

Hitler's message found an accepting audience. After elections in 1932, the Nazis became the largest party in the German government but did not have an outright majority. In offering Hitler the chancellorship, President von

"**The man who founded the Third Reich, who ruled it ruthlessly and often with uncommon shrewdness, who led it to such dizzy heights and to such a sorry end, was a person of undoubted, if evil, genius.**"

—JOURNALIST WILLIAM L. SHIRER

Hindenburg clearly hoped that Hitler could be tamed.

Then on Monday, Feb. 27, 1933, four weeks after Hitler was sworn in as chancellor, an arson attack on the Reichstag—the Berlin seat of Germany's parliament—changed the political situation. The Nazis claimed that the fire was part of a communist plot and used the event as a pretext to pass the so-called Enabling Act, a law allowing Hitler to govern without parliamentary consent.

Now dictator, Hitler leapt into action. On April 1, 1933, the Nazi Party led a nationwide boycott of Jewish-owned businesses. On April 25, a national law was passed to restrict Jewish students from schools and universities in order to ease "overcrowding."

DEMOCRACY IN DISREPUTE

President Woodrow Wilson pledged to make the world "safe for democracy" when he took America into World War I in 1917. And in the 1920s, many Americans thought that is what had happened. In his 1921 book *Modern Democracies*, British academic and politician James Bryce proclaimed "the universal acceptance of democracy as the normal and natural form of government."

But across Europe the war had left many countries, like Germany, with feeble economies and unstable political structures. As liberal democracies sank into crisis, authoritarianism appeared as the wave of the future. In Italy, a young man named Benito Mussolini—a onetime socialist who, like Hitler, had been wounded in World War I— founded the Fascist Party and clawed his way to power. Mussolini was named to lead Italy's parliamentary government in 1922, but in 1925 a fascist state was proclaimed with Mussolini, as its leader, promising to restore Italy to the power and glory of the Roman Empire.

Hirohito, here in 1928, was emperor of Japan during WWII, but the amount of power that he truly held remains unclear.

A German bank filled with currency in 1923, as hyperinflation crippled the country.

The Nazis used the Reichstag fire in 1933 to give Hitler absolute power in Germany.

DEM DEUTSCHEN VOLKE

EMPIRE OF THE EAST

On the other side of the world, Japan was shaping its own future as an empire, intent on becoming a colonial power like those in Europe. Japan's feudal past had been abandoned and imperial rule restored in 1868 under Emperor Meiji, who led a more centralized, assertive state that looked hungrily at other countries as a source for the natural resources—rubber, iron and oil—needed to develop a modern industrial power. The result was a series of territorial conflicts with China and, in 1904, a bloody war with Russia that ended with a stunning Japanese victory.

During World War I, Japan sided with Britain, France and the U.S., and had been rewarded with Germany's colonial empire in the Pacific Ocean. But its quest for territory created concern among its erstwhile friends. In the 1920s the U.S. and Great Britain began to fortify their Pacific possessions, with Britain establishing a naval base at Singapore—a base the British called "the Gibraltar of the East."

In 1926, Hirohito became the 124th emperor of Japan. It was a time of tension within the country, which had suffered from natural disasters, including a devastating earthquake in Tokyo in 1923 and a sinking economy. Militant nationalist groups, many led by young army officers, pressured for further conquest, and on Sept. 18, 1931, an Imperial Japanese army invaded Manchuria, a contested region in what today is northeastern China.

A PLUNGE INTO WAR

In 1935, Mussolini began fulfilling his pledge to create a modern-day Roman Empire. On Oct. 3 he sent his armies to invade Ethiopia, one of the few countries in Africa not yet dominated by European colonial powers. The League of Nations, a precursor to the United Nations that was established after World War I, imposed sanctions, but they had little effect. By May of 1936, Ethiopia had been subjugated. But the winds of war were just beginning to gust.

In July 1936, the Spanish Civil War broke out, with Republican forces backing Spain's left-leaning elected government facing a revolt by the Nationalists, an alliance of conservative elements. Germany and Italy poured supplies to the Nationalists, while the Republicans received aid from the Soviet Union and international groups.

On July 7, 1937, while the Spanish Civil War was still raging, war erupted between Japan and China. Japan had steadily been building forces in China since invading Manchuria in 1931, and an incident between Chinese and Japanese soldiers near Beijing set off the conflict. By the end of 1938, Japan had captured large areas of northern China, and Chiang Kai-shek, the leader of the Republic of China, withdrew his government inland.

HITLER'S DEMANDS

Meanwhile, Hitler was intent on remaking Germany. Political opponents—liberals, socialists and communists—were killed, imprisoned in new concentration camps or exiled. Jews were stripped of their German citizenship, and the superiority of Aryan peoples was taught in classrooms. The gifts of National Socialism were underscored by the Kraft durch Freude (Strength Through Joy) organization, which provided affordable concerts, sporting

This Shanghai railroad station was devastated in 1937 after a Japanese air attack.

German troops march into Austria in 1938.

Republican forces await battle in 1936 during the Spanish Civil War.

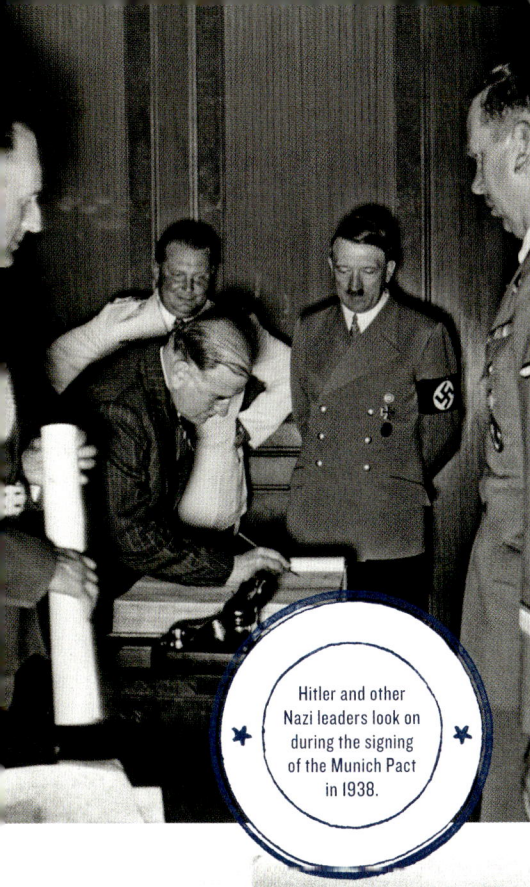

Hitler and other Nazi leaders look on during the signing of the Munich Pact in 1938.

activities and even a car for the masses—the KdF-Wagen—which eventually became known as the Volkswagen Beetle.

Germany also rearmed. In 1935, Hitler announced that the nation was building an air force and reinstituting conscription to create a large German army. The Spanish Civil War became a real-world testing ground for the weapons turned out by German factories. Those arms turned the tide of the war in favor of Spain's Nationalists.

Then Hitler began to take what he wanted. In March 1938, after delivering an ultimatum to Austria's chancellor, German troops entered that country. Next, Hitler turned his sights on Czechoslovakia and began threatening invasion.

In an attempt to avoid going to war, British Prime Minister Neville Chamberlain negotiated with Hitler, resulting in the Munich Pact. Signed in September 1938, it allowed Germany to annex the Sudetenland, a large portion of Czechoslovakia populated by German-speaking people. The führer had won Lebensraum and a prize rich in resources for his war machine, and he had done it without firing a shot.

Chamberlain, upon returning to London, proclaimed to cheers that the agreement brought "peace in our time." A year later, Europe would be at war. ⊕

Germany began to build concentration camps in 1933.

Winston Churchill's legendary speeches were written to raise morale at home while sending a message of defiance to Germany.

THE
LEADERS

IT IS IMPOSSIBLE TO LOOK BACK AT THE CALAMITY THAT BEFELL THE WORLD IN THE 1940S WITHOUT CONSIDERING THE MEN WHOSE DESIRE FOR CONQUEST LED THEIR COUNTRIES TO RUIN—AND THOSE WHO DEFIED THEM.

ADOLF HITLER

HIS DESTINY WAS GERMANY'S DESTINY.

OVER THE DECADES, he's been called a charlatan, a deranged genius and simply deranged. Whatever he was, Adolf Hitler brought about shattering violence such as the world had never seen.

He was born in obscurity, on the evening of April 20, 1889, in the Austrian town of Braunau am Inn, near the German border. The son of an Austrian customs official, he was, according to his half brother, quick to anger as a youth, often clashing with his father over his desire to become an artist. According to journalist William L. Shirer, the young Austrian developed a reverence for German culture early in his life, obsessing "that there should be no border between these two German-speaking peoples."

WOUNDED AND AGGRIEVED

In 1907, after his father's death, Hitler moved to the Austrian capital but was rejected as a student by Vienna's Academy of Fine Arts. He drifted to Munich and in 1914, with the outbreak of World War I, enlisted in the German army. In 1916 he was wounded at the Battle of the Somme, and in 1918 he was temporarily blinded by mustard gas. While recovering, he learned of Germany's defeat.

> **"God the Almighty has made our nation. By defending its existence we are defending His work."**
>
> —ADOLF HITLER, JANUARY 30, 1945

"His own personal failure," Winston Churchill would write later, "seems merged in the disaster of the whole German people." Hitler came to believe that Germany's military had been undone not on the battlefield, but rather by the maneuverings of politicians, Jews and Marxists.

THE HITLER MOVEMENT

With no other prospects, Hitler remained in the army after the war and was assigned to investigate a rowdy group in Munich called the German Workers' Party, the precursor of the Nazi Party. He saw opportunity in what he called an "absurd little organization," and by 1921 he was the party's chairman.

By 1932, the "Hitler movement," as one journalist noted at the time, had "ceased to be the frothy ebullition of irresponsible young men." By 1933, Hitler was Germany's führer.

DARK AND DEPRAVED

History has set aside a special place for Hitler as the personification of evil. And there have been no shortage of theories as to the root of that nefariousness—his grandfather was Jewish, he had syphilis, he was secretly gay, and more. Medical records indicate only that he stood 5 feet, 10 inches tall and weighed 150 pounds, that he neither drank nor smoked, and that he stuck to a strict vegetarian diet. He suffered from chronic constipation and diarrhea as well as arteriosclerotic heart disease and Parkinson's disease.

COCAINE AND OPIOIDS

Hitler complained of constant colds and insomnia. For stamina he was given vitamins and a methamphetamine called Pervitin. In his 2017 book, *Blitzed*, German writer Norman Ohler reported that Hitler grew dependent on a mix of cocaine and opioids during the course of the war.

Only Hitler's inner circle knew about his 14-year relationship with Eva Braun, whom he met when Braun was 17. As Hitler's mistress, Braun lived luxuriously at the Berghof, Hitler's home in the Bavarian Alps. The nature of their relationship—some who observed the couple claim it was platonic—has remained a mystery, along with so much else in Hitler's life.

A failed artist, Adolf Hitler became the unlikely master of Europe, then led his country to ruin.

BENITO MUSSOLINI

ITALY'S BOASTFUL IL DUCE.

Benito Mussolini
founded Italy's
National Fascist
Party in 1921.

BORN ON JULY 29, 1883, in the small town of Predappio, Italy, Benito Mussolini initially gained reknown as socialist journalist. He fought with the Italian army in World War I and returned home with a new vision of the future. Italy, he said, needed a "ruthless and energetic" dictator—himself.

RISE TO POWER
To back his ascent, Mussolini formed the fasci di combattimento, a violent paramilitary force. In 1922, he was named prime minister, but by 1928 he had taken absolute control of Italy as Il Duce, the leader.

WAR LEGACY
In 1939, Italy and Germany signed the so-called Pact of Steel, and in 1940 Mussolini joined the war as Hitler's Axis partner. After the Allies invaded Italy in 1943, Mussolini was ousted from power by his fascist compatriots and imprisoned. Rescued by German paratroopers, he then led a puppet regime backed by the German army.

In April 1945, with defeat imminent, Mussolini and his mistress were captured and executed by Italian partisans. Their bodies were taken to Milan and hung upside down from the roof of a gas station.

HIDEKI TOJO

THE FACE OF JAPANESE MILITARISM.

Hideki Tojo was bullish on preemptively attacking the United States and Europe.

AFTER GERMANY'S CONQUEST of France in 1940, Japan's war minister, Hideki Tojo, urged his government to take control of resource-rich colonial outposts in Southeast Asia. "We should not miss the present opportunity or we shall be blamed by posterity," he said. Tojo would end up being blamed for much worse.

GAINING STRENGTH

Born on Dec. 30, 1884, Tojo began his military career in 1905, going on to become Japan's war minister. He supported the Tripartite Pact, a defensive agreement between Germany, Italy and Japan that was signed in September 1940. When mounting pressure with the military led to the fall of Japanese Prime Minister Fumimaro Konoe, Tojo replaced him and became Japan's virtual dictator in October 1940.

SEEKING DOMINANCE

Tojo backed the bombing of Pearl Harbor and conquered vast areas of the Pacific and Southeast Asia, where he presided over the massacre and starvation of civilians and prisoners of war. When the island of Saipan fell in July 1944, Tojo's government collapsed. Following Japan's surrender, he was tried and executed as a war criminal in 1945.

WINSTON CHURCHILL

HE WAS RESOLUTE IN BRITAIN'S DARKEST HOUR.

BRITISH PRIME MINISTER Winston Churchill once said of himself, "We are all worms. But I do believe I am a glowworm." Others saw him in differing ways. "Temperamental as a film star and peevish as a spoilt child," one underling wrote of him. "In great things he is very great," said an admiring friend. "In small things not great."

His greatness sprang from words. During his life, Churchill authored 58 books—including seven books of memoir and 16 volumes of history—but his most enduring words were those he spoke when Great Britain was left all but defenseless in the face of German might in 1940.

Addressing the House of Commons on June 4, 1940, after the British Expeditionary Force had been driven from France, Churchill vowed that Great Britain would fight on, "if necessary for years, if necessary alone." He vowed to do battle on the seas and oceans, in the air, on the beaches, on the landing grounds, in the streets and fields and in the hills. "We shall never surrender," he said.

> **"All the greatest things are simple, and many can be expressed in a single word: freedom; justice; honour; duty; mercy; hope."**
>
> —WINSTON CHURCHILL

"I SHALL SAVE LONDON"

Churchill was born in Oxfordshire on Nov. 30, 1874, to a wealthy, powerful family. His paternal grandfather, John Spencer-Churchill, 7th Duke of Marlborough, had been a Conservative member of Parliament, as was his father, Lord Randolph Churchill. His mother, Jennie, came from a moneyed American family.

By his own admission, Churchill hated school and was a poor pupil, until he found what interested him: "French, history, lots of poetry by heart, and above all riding and swimming." He had a vision of his own destiny. A childhood friend would later recall a conversation he had with Churchill, who predicted for himself a life of "great adventures" and foresaw a day when England would be under threat.

"I tell you I shall be in command of the defenses of London and I shall save London from disaster," he said.

POLITICAL POWERHOUSE

The adventures began after Churchill left the Sandhurst military academy and traveled across the British Empire as a soldier and journalist. By 26, he had published five books. In 1900 he joined the House of Commons, and by 1911 he was First Lord of the Admiralty. During World War I, his proposed Allied invasion of the Gallipoli Peninsula in Turkey turned into a disaster costing 250,000 casualties. Churchill resigned his post, became an officer in the army and served on the front in France until early 1916.

As a member of Parliament in the 1930s, Churchill repeatedly warned of Adolf Hitler's rise and Germany's rearmament, even as Prime Minister Neville Chamberlain

Taken prisoner while reporting on the Boer War in South Africa, Winston Churchill escaped and traveled 300 miles to freedom.

CHURCHILL AND ROOSEVELT
THE MEETING THAT SHAPED THE WAR

With many friendly nations under German occupation, Great Britain had largely faced Hitler's army alone until Dec. 7, 1941, when Japan's attack on Pearl Harbor took America to war in both the Pacific and Europe. Winston Churchill rejoiced knowing he at last had a partner in the fight. "Being saturated and satiated with emotion and sensation, I went to bed and slept the sleep of the saved and thankful," he wrote later.

Soon after the U.S. entered the war, Churchill traveled across the Atlantic to meet with President Franklin D. Roosevelt. Two weeks after the Pearl Harbor attack, he was in Washington for a three-week stay—though Roosevelt told his surprised wife, Eleanor, that the prime minister would be visiting for just "a few days."

Once settled in the White House, the 67-year-old Churchill made clear his needs—"a tumbler of sherry in my room before breakfast, a couple of glasses of scotch and soda before lunch and French champagne, and 90-year-old brandy before I go to sleep at night."

The president and prime minister sketched out strategies that shaped the war, with Roosevelt agreeing the U.S. would prioritize the defeat of the Axis Powers. Still, the visit wasn't without its tribulations. After speaking before Congress on Dec. 26, Churchill suffered a mild heart attack, which he kept secret. The trip also left the president's staff exhausted; one Roosevelt adviser checked into a hospital to recover.

mistakenly thought he could negotiate his way to peace with Hitler. On Sept. 3, 1939, the day Britain declared war on Germany, Chamberlain named Churchill First Lord of the Admiralty once more.

After the Allied forces failed to stop the German invasion of Norway, the House of Commons held the Norway Debate, after which Chamberlain resigned. Grudgingly respected by both the Labour and Conservative parties, Churchill became prime minister in May 1940. "I have nothing to offer but blood, toil, tears and sweat," he said in his first speech as PM.

He led the nation through the war, but was relegated to minority leader when Conservatives lost power in 1944. In 1951, he led them back to power and served as PM, until ill health forced him to resign in 1955.

LEGACY OF WORDS

Journalist Edward R. Murrow, who reported from London during the war, would later say Churchill "mobilized the English language and sent it into battle." In 1963, a year before Churchill's death at 90, President John F. Kennedy quoted Murrow when he made Churchill an honorary American citizen.

Churchill and President Roosevelt discuss strategy at the White House in late 1941.

FRANKLIN D. ROOSEVELT

THE MASTER POLITICIAN TRIUMPHED OVER ADVERSITY.

FRANKLIN DELANO ROOSEVELT, 32nd president of the United States, had a trick for falling asleep on nights when tensions and concern over the day's events left him wakeful. In her book about the Roosevelt White House years, *No Ordinary Time*, historian Doris Kearns Goodwin noted that the president would close his eyes and imagine himself as a boy at his home in Hyde Park, New York, climbing hills and sledding in the snowy landscape of the Hudson Valley. With that memory, the problems of the nation and the world drifted away, as did the awareness of his shrunken legs, wasted by polio.

He must have had many such nights. In March 1933, Roosevelt became the leader of a country in the depths of depression and then transformed America with his New Deal economic policies. By his second term, he was warning Americans about dangers from abroad—the rise of fascism in Europe and militarism in Japan. In 1940, he was reelected to an unprecedented third term,

> **"Roosevelt's wartime diplomacy paved the way for the defeat of the Axis Powers and the establishment of a world order based on the rule of law."**
>
> —BIOGRAPHER JEAN EDWARD SMITH

promising Americans that he would keep the country out of the war in Europe. He then deftly outmaneuvered isolationist politicians to help arm Great Britain and the Soviet Union.

And when the nation entered the war in December 1941, Roosevelt, who'd prevailed over paralysis and economic collapse, had a new role: leader of the free world.

FAMILY TIES

Franklin D. Roosevelt entered the national political scene with powerful name recognition. Born on Jan. 30, 1882, the only child of James and Sara Delano Roosevelt, he was a fifth cousin to Theodore

Roosevelt, the 26th president. While attending Harvard University, Franklin fell in love with Theodore's niece (and his own distant cousin) Anna Eleanor Roosevelt, and they married in 1905.

Following in Theodore Roosevelt's political footsteps, Franklin served as assistant secretary of the U.S. Navy during World War I, and in 1920 he was the Democratic Party's nominee for vice president. Though the Democrats lost the election, Roosevelt's career profited. Then, in 1921, at the age of 39, he was vacationing with family at Campobello, a Canadian island off the coast of Maine, when he fell ill with polio.

Paralyzed from the waist down, he was urged by his mother to retire from public life. Eleanor, however, convinced Roosevelt to persevere, and herself became a powerful speaker on his behalf.

REEMERGENCE

Roosevelt focused on physical rehabilitation and by 1922 was

"Great power involves great responsibility," Franklin D. Roosevelt said during his last address to the nation.

able to stand with leg braces. He traveled to Warm Springs, Georgia, for therapy in the spring's mineral waters and ended up buying the resort and establishing a rehabilitation center there for fellow polio patients.

In 1924, he reemerged on the political scene when he appeared at the Democratic National Convention to nominate New York Governor Al Smith for president. Smith lost the nomination, and unsuccessfully ran again four years later. That same year, 1928, Franklin D. Roosevelt was elected governor of New York.

NOTHING TO FEAR

With America's economic woes growing after the 1929 Wall Street crash, Roosevelt ran for president against unpopular incumbent Herbert Hoover in 1932 and won in a landslide, carrying all but six states and taking 57% of the popular vote. In his 1933 inaugural address, Roosevelt reassured Americans that the nation would "endure as it had endured." The only thing they had to fear, he said, was fear itself.

Both the nation and his words did endure. With his series of aggressive social programs, Roosevelt greatly expanded the role of the federal government and pulled the U.S. out of depression. And of course he was instrumental in bringing down the Axis Powers in WWII. He's largely regarded as one of the country's greatest leaders. When Roosevelt died of a massive stroke in April 1945, his longtime political nemesis, isolationist Republican Sen. Robert Taft, called him "the greatest figure of our time."

Roosevelt was reluctant to bring the country into war until the bombing of Pearl Harbor forced his hand.

HARRY TRUMAN

THE QUIET MAN'S BIG MOMENT.

IN 1940, ROOSEVELT broke with a tradition set by George Washington (and later mandated by the 22nd Amendment) by running for a third term as president. By 1944, with America in the midst of a global war, he campaigned for a fourth term with running mate Harry S. Truman, an unassuming senator from Missouri.

The war had clearly taken a toll on the 62-year-old Roosevelt. In late March he left Washington for his retreat in Warm Springs, Georgia, and there, on the afternoon of April 12, he complained of a "terrific pain" in his head and died from a brain hemorrhage.

SURPRISING ASCENT

Vice President Truman, a former county judge and U.S. senator who had never graduated from college, unexpectedly became the nation's new leader. He told reporters that he felt "like the moon, the stars and all the planets had fallen on me."

The responsibility of ending the war also fell to Truman. On April 26, he was told the full details of the Manhattan Project, the United States' attempt to build an atomic bomb. Less than four months later, he used that bomb against Japan, forcing their surrender.

In the years since he left office, Harry Truman (here in 1945) has grown in esteem.

Postwar, Truman faced the growing expansion of communism and the Cold War with the Soviet Union. Still, he edged out Republican Thomas Dewey to win another term as president in 1948.

As tensions escalated, he sent troops into Korea in 1950. With the war still raging, his popularity plummeted and he didn't run for another full term in 1952. He died on Christmas Day 1972 at age 88.

JOSEPH STALIN

A TYRANT BECOMES AN ALLY AGAINST HITLER.

ON JUNE 22, 1941, the war took a turn when, without warning, Adolf Hitler launched Operation Barbarossa, invading the Soviet Union with 3.8 million troops supported by planes and tanks. Suddenly, Soviet dictator Joseph Stalin, who had signed a nonaggression treaty with Hitler just 22 months before, was an ally against Germany.

For Winston Churchill, there was no alternative but to embrace the Communist tyrant whose reign of terror had led to the deaths of millions of his own people. Speaking on the radio, Churchill affirmed he was a foe of communism. "But," he said, "all this fades away before the spectacle which is now unfolding.... Any man or state who fights on against Nazidom will have our aid."

Four days after the invasion, German tanks had pushed deep into Soviet territory, two Russian armies were destroyed, and 600,000 Soviet prisoners had been taken. Stalin ordered Soviet soldiers caught retreating be placed in "penal battalions" and used as cannon fodder, as they fought on.

MAN OF STEEL

Joseph Vissarionovich Dzhugashvili was born on Dec. 18, 1878, in the Georgian town of Gori, then part of the Russian Empire. His father was a cobbler who drank and beat him, and his mother, a devout Orthodox Christian, wanted him to be a priest. He did well at school, where he learned to speak Russian, and earned a scholarship to the Tiflis Theological Seminary. There he wrote poetry, became involved with a group advocating Georgia's independence from Russia and secretly read socialist theoretician Karl Marx's *Das Kapital*.

Abandoning the priesthood, he got into revolutionary politics and became a follower of Vladimir Lenin's Bolsheviks. He performed various roles—from leading strikes to raising money through robbery, counterfeiting and kidnapping—and was repeatedly arrested and exiled to Siberia. Along the way he changed his name to Stalin, derived from the Russian word for steel.

POWER AND PURGE

Stalin escaped exile just in time for the 1917 Russian Revolution that brought the Bolsheviks to power. With Lenin's support he became secretary general of the Communist Party's Central Committee and began consolidating power. After Lenin's death in 1924, Stalin took sole control of the Soviet Union.

Stalin launched state-organized industrialization on a massive scale and forced millions of peasants onto collective farms, causing a famine that took 5 million to 10 million lives.

The 1934 assassination of Sergei Kirov, a prominent member of the Communist Party—and potential Stalin rival—led to the Great Purge, or Great Terror, a campaign of political suppression involving the ethnic cleansing of minorities and the elimination of political opponents by execution and imprisonment in Siberian forced labor camps, or gulags. According to estimates, the Great Terror led to the deaths of more than a million people.

DICTATOR VS. DICTATOR

Stalin's 1939 pact with Hitler allowed the Soviet Union to annex eastern Poland and other territories, while Hitler took the rest of Poland. But the partnership could not last.

Stalin's forces met Hitler's invasion with a disorganized response, in part because purges had removed experienced leaders. By winter 1941, the German army was nearing Moscow. But Stalin outlasted Hitler; the Soviet Army stormed Berlin in 1945. Stalin ruled over a new Soviet empire until his death from a stroke in 1953. ⊕

A former seminary student, Joseph Stalin embraced revolutionary politics, and war, with ruthlessness.

The U.S. Army's Sherman tank was reliable and cheap to produce but also vulnerable.

WEAPONS
OF WAR

EARLY ON IN THE CONFLICT, THE ALLIES
LAGGED IN MILITARY TECHNOLOGY,
BUT THEY SOON FIELDED AN ADVANCED
ARSENAL ON SEA, LAND AND AIR.

Servicemen work on a
Vought F4U Corsair,
an aircraft carrier-
based fighter.

IN LATE 1941 and early 1942, as its forces swept across the Pacific, Japan ruled the skies, thanks in no small part to the Mitsubishi A6M Zero, a single-seat fighter plane that had been designed to outclimb and outmaneuver any other fighter aircraft of the era.

"Allied pilots who survived their initial dogfighting or 'tail-chasing' contests with the Zero were staggered by the machine's capacity to turn sharply and climb away at high speed," noted author and historian Ian W. Toll in *The Conquering Tide*, his 2015 history of the Pacific War.

Two years later, the fearsome Zero was outmatched by a new generation of U.S. aircraft, most notably the Grumman F6F Hellcat, a heavily armored aircraft carrier–based fighter powered by an enormous 2,000-horsepower engine. The rugged plane could outclimb the Zero at high altitudes and outrace it in level flight and in dives.

As the U.S. pressed its counterattack in the central Pacific, it did so with what amounted to a new Navy—bigger, more powerful aircraft carriers and planes like the Hellcat, the Grumman TBF Avenger torpedo bomber and the Vought F4U Corsair fighter. In mid-June of 1944, as U.S. forces moved into the Mariana Islands, Japan's front line of defense, the Japanese navy aimed for a decisive naval battle and got it—the Battle of the Philippine Sea, during which U.S. Navy aviators shot down so many Japanese aircraft with so little loss of their own that the episode came to be known as the Great Marianas Turkey Shoot. The Zero was the turkey.

MESSERSCHMITT BF 109

MITSUBISHI A6M ZERO

The British Hawker Hurricane (below) accounted for over 60% of the air victories in the Battle of Britain.

The victory over Japan's great fighter plane is just one example of how the Allies overcame early losses in both Europe and the Pacific by fielding an ever-improving arsenal— from ships and submarines to aircraft, tanks, artillery and small arms—that turned the tide of battle.

SHATTERED ILLUSIONS

The victors of World War I didn't expect to begin fighting again so soon. Consequently, they went into World War II with weapons that, in many cases, hadn't changed much since 1918. The British spent relatively little on military research and development, while the French bet on the Maginot Line, a series of border fortifications meant to stop German troops. Not anticipated was Germany's blitzkrieg, or lightning war, which used fast-moving concentrations of Panzer tanks,

VOUGHT F4U CORSAIR

The Grumman F6F Hellcat had the highest kill-to-loss ratio of any U.S. plane in WWII— about 19-to-1.

GERMAN PANZER TANK

mobile infantry and air support to roll past defenses.

In the Pacific, Britain and the U.S. allowed what Toll calls "hubris and racial chauvinism" to lead them into a serious misjudgment of Japan's military technology.

"Before December 1941," noted Toll in *The Conquering Tide*, "American and British aviation experts insisted that Japanese airplanes were poorly designed knockoffs of Western technology,

and Japanese pilots were considered laughably inept crash-test dummies." After the Pearl Harbor attack, those illusions were shattered.

THE BATTLE ABOVE

In Europe, Germany learned valuable lessons about the effectiveness of its newly designed weaponry during the Spanish Civil War. The Nazis' Junkers Ju 87, better known as the Stuka dive

bomber, went into combat in 1937 in support of Spain's Nationalists. Infamous for its near-vertical diving attacks and the terrifying howl it produced with propeller-driven sirens, the Stuka was a key part of the Nazi invasion of Poland in 1939 and its conquest of the Netherlands, Belgium and France in 1940.

The Stuka's usefulness faded as it began to face better Allied fighters. But another Nazi plane that debuted in the Spanish Civil War—the

JUNKERS JU 87

GRUMMAN TBF AVENGER

SPITFIRE

Messerschmitt Bf 109—would become a mainstay of the German Luftwaffe throughout the war.

During the Battle of Britain, however, it met its match with Britain's Supermarine Spitfire. A short-range interceptor aircraft, the Spitfire's elliptical wing design helped make it almost as fast as the Messerschmitt, but more maneuverable. It defended Britain's skies with the more numerous but slower Hawker Hurricane fighter.

The Spitfire's qualities earned admiration from those who faced it in combat. When Hermann Goering, head of the Luftwaffe, asked one of his pilots what he needed to beat the British, the man sarcastically said "an outfit of Spitfires."

AIR SUPERIORITY

By 1942, another airplane began making history when the first Boeing B-17 Flying Fortress arrived in Great Britain to join

the U.S. Army Air Corps' Eighth Air Force. The B-17, a four-engine long-range bomber bristling with five .30-caliber machine guns for defense, was developed in the late 1930s and first deployed in the Pacific. It underwent a number of design evolutions before earning a reputation for toughness during daylight bombing raids over German targets.

As the air war over Europe progressed, the B-17s were escorted on their missions by the P-51 Mustang. A long-range fighter and fighter-bomber designed in 1940 under a commission for Britain's Royal Air Force, the American-built P-51 was initially underpowered and used mostly for reconnaissance. When it was married to a Rolls-Royce Merlin engine, its role changed. As an escort for the B-17s, it outmatched Germany's best fighters.

By 1944, the P-51 was not merely escorting bombers, but sweeping the skies ahead of them and attacking the Luftwaffe relentlessly. The tactic helped the Allies achieve air superiority in Europe prior to the D-Day invasion of France in 1944.

VICTORY AT SEA

In the Pacific, Allied air power was projected across the vast ocean by aircraft carriers. Japan began the war with the largest and most modern carrier fleet in the world, and its raid on Pearl Harbor, with more than 350 aircraft attacking from six carriers, showed how effective they could be. The U.S. lost four battleships in the attack, but the Navy's three Pacific carriers—the *Enterprise*, *Lexington* and *Saratoga*—were all at sea during the attack and survived.

U.S. and Japanese carriers met the following May during the Battle of the Coral Sea—the first naval battle in which opposing ships neither sighted nor fired directly on one another. Both sides suffered heavy damages. A month later, however, the U.S. won the Battle of Midway, with aircraft from three American carriers sinking four Japanese carriers. The U.S. lost just one, the USS *Yorktown*. (For more on the Battle of Midway, see page 108.)

HITS AND MISSES
RADAR AND THE NORDEN BOMBSIGHT

The World War II Allies produced military technology that led to victory and shaped the future. But there were expensive misses as well.

Effective radar gave the Royal Air Force a vital edge over the Luftwaffe during the Battle of Britain. Initially, Scottish engineer Robert Watson-Watt was asked to create a "death ray" to take down the Luftwaffe, but he instead developed a way to focus a radar beam on an object. The beam would rebound, revealing the object's location and altitude.

Germany also knew about radar, but put a greater effort into building other types of weapons. The U.S. started the war with far less advanced radar technology but learned how vital it could be after the Japanese attacked Pearl Harbor. Later, more sophisticated radar would change the way battles in the Pacific were fought.

One technology the U.S. did back was a bombsight invented by Dutch-born engineer Carl Norden. The Norden bombsight—essentially an analog computer—was built in great secrecy and at an enormous cost: more than a billion dollars (in 1940s dollars), about half of what was spent on the Manhattan Project. Using Norden's invention, a bombardier in a plane would visually sight a target, plug in available data such as altitude and speed, and find out when the plane should drop its payload of bombs.

The promise was pinpoint accuracy, but the Norden bombsight didn't deliver. It was complicated to use and needed cloudless skies to work, which proved to be a major drawback. The Air Force ended up turning away from precision bombing in favor of area bombing in order to hit its targets.

M1 GARAND

The Gato–class submarine USS *Wahoo* was launched on Feb. 14, 1942.

The Essex-class aircraft carrier USS *Bunker Hill* was hit by kamikaze attacks in 1945.

Japan's industry could not easily replace those losses. The U.S. could, and by 1943 the U.S. Navy had a new kind of carrier—the Essex class. These giants held more than 90 aircraft, including the F6F Hellcat, were equipped with sophisticated radar and tore through seas at 33 knots. In 1944, Essex-class carriers devastated the Japanese navy in the Battle of the Philippine Sea and the Battle of Leyte Gulf, the largest naval battle of World War II.

UNDERWATER DOMINANCE

For all the might of the new aircraft carriers, it was U.S. submarines that were responsible for more than half of the Japanese naval tonnage that was sunk during the war. By 1945, submarines had put a stranglehold on Japan's vital lifeline to raw materials and food.

The machine behind this nautical carnage was the Gato-class sub. A little more than 311 feet in length, these submarines were powered by four diesel engines on the surface and four electric motors when they went below. They could dive to 300 feet, stay submerged for 48 hours and remain on patrol for 75 days.

Inside, crews of six officers and 54 enlisted men enjoyed such luxuries as air-conditioning, freshwater distilling units and clothes washers. Each crewman had his own bunk.

Early on in the Pacific War, problems beset the American submarines. Their commanders

The P-51 Mustang was initially underpowered but later became a fearsome fighter-bomber.

Soviet T-34 tanks cut a commanding presence.

German Tiger tanks show their stripes.

had yet to develop effective tactics, and torpedoes often malfunctioned. Gradually, the Navy improved the torpedoes and put subs under the command of audacious young officers. As better radar and sonar systems were added, the Gato-class submarine became a lethal weapon.

ON THE BATTLEGROUND

According to Gen. George Patton, the most important weapon of the war was neither plane nor ship. In a letter to the Army's chief of ordnance, Patton praised the M1 Garand—the standard U.S. service rifle—as "the greatest battle implement ever derived."

The .30-06-caliber semi-automatic rifle's primary attribute was firepower: The U.S. was the only country to equip its soldiers with standard autoloading rifles, giving them an advantage over enemies firing slower bolt-action weapons. The M1 was also easy to assemble and disassemble in the field.

In his letter, Patton went on to praise American machine guns, mortars, artillery and tanks, which, he said, were "without equal on the battlefields of the world."

TANK WARFARE

Crewmen in a U.S. Army M4 Sherman tank might have disagreed with Patton. The Sherman, reliable and cheap to produce, was the most widely used light tank in the Allied arsenal. It first saw combat in North Africa in 1942 and, with its 75 mm gun and maneuverability, it held its own against German Panzer tanks.

When the Allies invaded Europe in 1944, they found the Sherman outgunned by new German Tiger tanks, whose 88 mm cannon could punch through the Sherman's comparatively light armor, setting it ablaze. Tank crews gave the Sherman a nickname—the Ronson, because, like the cigarette lighter, "it lights up the first time, every time."

Perhaps the most formidable tank of the war was the Soviet T-34, which picked off German Panzers with a 76.2 mm high-velocity cannon, while its sloped armor was difficult to penetrate. When the Germans fielded more powerful tanks, the T-34 was upgraded with a larger 85 mm gun. Upon first encountering the T-34 in 1941, German Gen. Paul Ludwig von Kleist called it "the finest tank in the world." ⊕

Workers at the Los Alamos complex prepare to test an atomic bomb.

THE RACE FOR SUPERWEAPONS

WORRIED ABOUT NAZI SCIENTIFIC ADVANCEMENTS,
U.S. PRESIDENT FRANKLIN D. ROOSEVELT LAUNCHED
AN ALL-OUT EFFORT TO BUILD AN ATOMIC BOMB.
BUT ADOLF HITLER PREFERRED OTHER TECHNOLOGY.

WRITING IN HIS diary on March 21, 1942, Nazi propaganda minister Joseph Goebbels noted that he had received an optimistic report about work German scientists were doing on a new kind of weapon.

"Research in the realm of atomic destruction," he wrote, "has now proceeded to a point where its results may possibly be made use of in the conduct of this war. Tremendous destruction, it is claimed, can be wrought with a minimum of effort." Goebbels, one of Adolf Hitler's closest associates, added developments showed "German science at its best."

Nazi work on atomic weaponry had begun in 1939, shortly after the discovery of nuclear fission by German scientists Otto Hahn and Fritz Strassmann. But news of the discovery, and its theoretical implications, did not remain confined to Germany. The scientific community in America, which included a number of physicists who had fled Hitler's Europe, soon learned of the breakthrough.

One of them, Albert Einstein, wrote a letter to President Franklin D. Roosevelt noting that the discovery by Hahn and Strassmann, combined with work being done in America by Italian émigré scientist Enrico Fermi and Hungarian physicist Leo Szilard, showed it was possible to make a bomb of colossal power.

The letter was delivered to Roosevelt by economist Alexander Sachs in October 1939. At first, the president was skeptical the physicists' theories could be turned into a weapon, but, pressed by Sachs, he soon came to understand the urgency of the matter. "Alex, what you are after is to see that the Nazis don't blow us up," Roosevelt said. "This requires action."

THE FÜHRER'S FALLACIES

The president's decision that day would lead to a massive endeavor that, by 1945, would employ more than 120,000 people and cost $2 billion—$28 billion in today's dollars. It would end with the destruction of two Japanese cities, the end of the war, and the birth of a decades-long cold war.

The Nazi threat that focused Roosevelt's resolve, on the other hand, proved to be a halting effort. Germany's program to build an atomic bomb was sidelined by other military aims and Nazi policies that undermined Germany's quest for dominance in weaponry. Following Hitler's rise in 1933, many scientists and engineers fled Germany. Many who remained were drafted into the armed forces, while Jewish scientists were purged from universities.

Early work by German scientists in the spring of 1939 was abandoned after the invasion of Poland only months later. Another program was launched with the goal of creating a nuclear reactor, but midway through the war, as millions of German troops fought in the vastness of the Soviet Union, work was scaled back. Nazi policy makers determined that nuclear fission wouldn't significantly contribute to the war's end.

It wasn't a hard decision to make: Hitler, who disparaged nuclear science as "Jewish physics," wasn't interested in an atomic bomb.

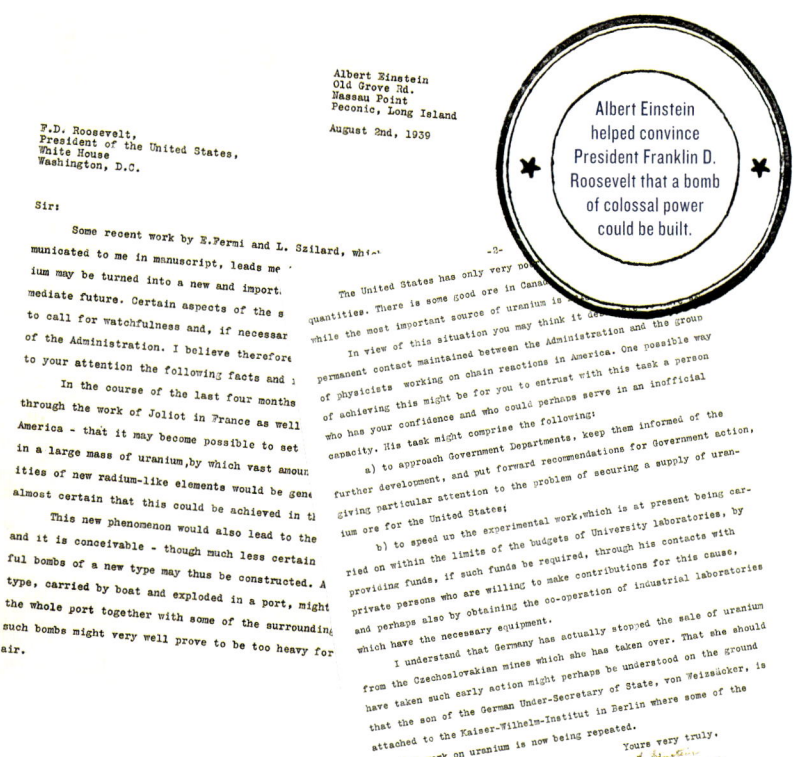

Albert Einstein helped convince President Franklin D. Roosevelt that a bomb of colossal power could be built.

Workers arrive at the Manhattan Project's top-secret Oak Ridge Facility.

A sign at the Oak Ridge Facility warns workers to keep silent.

WHAT YOU SEE HERE
WHAT YOU DO HERE
WHAT YOU HEAR HERE
WHEN YOU LEAVE HERE
LET IT STAY HERE

MANHATTAN PROJECT
A BOMB

BRITAIN'S "TUBE ALLOYS"

By contrast, Roosevelt established the Advisory Committee on Uranium, which was composed of both scientists and military officials. Based on the committee's findings, the U.S. began funding early research in 1940.

By early 1942, with the U.S. at war with Germany and Japan, Roosevelt and British Prime Minister Winston Churchill had agreed to cooperate on the development of an atomic bomb: The British had been secretly working on atomic weaponry through a project code-named Tube Alloys, but with Britain under constant attack by Germany, it had become too risky to continue the research. Meeting with Roosevelt at his home in Hyde Park, New York, in June 1942, Churchill was relieved when the president said that the United States would take the lead in developing an atomic weapon.

THE MANHATTAN PROJECT

Two months later, Roosevelt launched the Manhattan Project, named for the New York City borough where initial work was done. Led by U.S. Army Gen. Leslie Groves, the massive effort sprawled out across the country, from the University of Chicago, where Fermi successfully created a sustained nuclear reaction in December 1942, to top-secret uranium and plutonium production facilities at Oak Ridge, Tennessee, and Hanford, Washington.

Los Alamos, a remote settlement in northern New Mexico, was chosen as the site for what was called Project Y—a complex where many of the world's foremost scientists gathered under strict security to design and build an atomic bomb.

They were led by theoretical physicist Robert Oppenheimer, who had been exploring the possibility of developing an atomic weapon while at the University of California, Berkeley. Oppenheimer and Groves formed an unlikely but effective association. Groves, an Army engineer, could be abrasive and sarcastic, but he saw in the charismatic Oppenheimer a genius of "overweening ambition" who was determined to leave his mark on science and history.

"WUNDERWAFFEN"

Adolf Hitler may not have fully appreciated the value of nuclear science, but he did want to possess wunderwaffen—"wonder weapons"—and Nazi engineers created a variety of futuristic military technologies, including the Fritz X, the world's first radio-guided bomb used in combat, and the Messerschmitt Me 163 Komet, the first rocket-powered fighter aircraft. Introduced in combat in 1944, the Komet pushed its pilots' skills to the limit. Ultimately, however, the plane was considered a failure by the Luftwaffe, which favored an easier-to-fly jet-powered fighter, the Messerschmitt Me 262.

Hitler also had an early cruise missile, the V-1 flying bomb, often called the buzz bomb by Allies because of the distinctive sound made by its pulse-jet engine. The "V" in the name stood for Vergeltungswaffe—"vengeance weapon": Hitler rained thousands of the bombs on England after the D-Day invasion of Normandy. But the buzz bomb was often inaccurate and, though terrifying to Londoners, did nothing to stop the Allies' advance across France.

The German Messerschmitt Me 163 Komet was the first rocket-powered fighter aircraft.

NEW WORLD

Neither did the V-2 rocket, the world's first long-range guided ballistic missile and the Nazis' most advanced weapon. Hitler's rockets, jet aircraft and guided bombs were rushed into the war while such technology was still experimental. Given time, Nazi engineers would certainly have perfected the weapons. But in the early months of 1945, time was a luxury the Nazis did not have.

As Allied armies pushed into Germany from both the west and the east, the search was on for the secrets of advanced Nazi technology—especially the rocketry of the V-2 missile. The Soviets began rounding up German rocket scientists, and the U.S. launched Operation Paperclip, which secretly sent some 1,600 German scientists and engineers—including Dr. Wernher von Braun, the chief designer of the V-2—to America. Von Braun would go on to design the rockets that took American astronauts to the moon.

Meanwhile, in New Mexico, Oppenheimer's team of scientists were getting ready to test the bomb they'd been working on since 1943. On May 7, 1945, the day Germany officially surrendered, they exploded 91 tons of TNT in order to calibrate sensitive measuring devices.

Two months later, at 5:29 a.m. on July 16, they successfully detonated what they called their "gadget" in the New Mexico desert. The new atomic age had begun. ⊕

Gen. Leslie Groves led the massive Manhattan Project, which employed 120,000 people.

Physicist Robert Oppenheimer (left) worked closely alongside Groves.

The Gustave Gun was the opposite of portable.

HITLER'S WEIRDEST WARCRAFT

WAR DRIVES INNOVATION, AND THERE SEEMED TO BE NO END OF IT AMONG NAZI ENGINEERS. HERE ARE A FEW OF THEIR MORE EXOTIC INVENTIONS

The Gustave Gun

Delivered to the German army in 1941, the Gustave Gun was the largest piece of artillery ever used in battle. The four-story, 155-foot-long gun shot 10,000-pound shells from a 98-foot barrel. It could be transported only by railway, making it an easy target for Allied aircraft. It was dropped within a year.

The V-3 "Busy Lilly" Cannon

Devised in 1944 to fire artillery shells from France to London, the V-3 supergun was so big—about 430 feet in length—that it had to be built on a hillside to support its own weight. It was soon scrapped.

The Amerika Bomber

Adolf Hitler wanted to see New York City in flames, so the Nazis developed a long-range bomber (right) capable of making a round-trip flight from Germany to the U.S. A prototype was built, and there are reports of long-range Amerika Bomber flights, but the mammoth plane was judged to be a costly, ill-conceived mistake.

The Krummlauf Curved Gun Barrel

An example of Germany's obsession with experimental weapons in the war's final years, the Krummlauf was a curved barrel attachment for the Sturmgewehr 44 (StG 44) assault rifle that enabled it to be fired around corners. It performed poorly for a variety of reasons. Development of such outlandish weapons diverted critical resources from more effective technology.

CHAPTER 2

THE EUROPEAN THEATER

SOON AFTER GERMANY INVADED POLAND IN 1939, THE
CONTINENT WAS THRUST INTO HEAVY FIGHTING THAT WOULD
NOT COME TO A BLOODY END FOR SIX LONG, HARD YEARS.

Germany invaded
Poland on Sept. 1,
1939, igniting
World War II.

EUROPE
IN
FLAMES

CRISIS, CONVICTION AND COURAGE,
FROM POLAND TO NORMANDY.

German troops invaded the Netherlands on their way to France in May 1940.

THE SECOND WORLD WAR began at dawn on Sept. 1, 1939, when 1.5 million German soldiers, 2,000 German airplanes and 2,500 German tanks smashed across the Polish border in a lightning attack.

The first strike, reported *Time* magazine 10 days later, came "when a German bombing plane dropped a projectile on Puck, [a] fishing village and air base in the armpit of the Hel Peninsula. At 5:45 a.m., the German training ship *Schleswig-Holstein* lying off Danzig fired what

was believed to be the first shell: a direct hit on the Polish underground ammunition dump at Westerplatte." The attack, the magazine's dispatch added, came on "a gray day, with gentle rain."

Germany's attack set off a crisis in Europe that had been brewing for a year. In September 1938, Adolf Hitler had signed the Munich Pact, allowing him to annex the German-speaking portion of Czechoslovakia in exchange for his promise not to invade any more territory. He broke

his pledge by marching troops into the rest of Czechoslovakia in March 1939. Britain and France responded by signing a military alliance with his likely next target—Poland.

Hitler, along with many Germans, resented the loss of territory to the Polish state created after World War I, and while he had signed a nonaggression pact with Poland in the 1930s, his promises were by this time more than suspect. His aims became more certain when, in August 1939, Germany and the Soviet Union signed a nonaggression agreement called the Molotov-Ribbentrop Pact. Just a week later, Germany launched its invasion from the west, and on Sept. 17, the Soviet Union invaded Poland from the east, dividing the country between them.

Honoring their pact with Poland, Britain and France declared war on Germany on Sept. 3.

BLITZKRIEG AND CONQUEST

For the moment, though, there was also no fighting. Over the next eight months, a period termed the "phony war" by journalists, Germany, Britain and France plotted their next moves. France hoped to remain safe behind its fortified Maginot Line, which ran along the French-German border. Crucially, however, the defensive system did not extend along the French-Belgian frontier. That, in May 1940, is where Germany struck.

In a bold plan devised by Gen. Erich von Manstein, German forces attacked through neutral Holland and Belgium, with the main blow coming unexpectedly through the heavily forested Ardennes region of southwest Belgium. Panzer tank divisions struck ahead of the main German army.

The attack began on May 10, and by May 14 the Netherlands had surrendered. Meanwhile, the Germans thrust through the Ardennes cutoff and surrounded Allied forces that had rushed into Belgium to meet the invasion there. Several hundred thousand British and French troops were pushed back to the coast of the English Channel in northern France.

THE DUNKIRK MIRACLE

There, in the coastal town of Dunkirk, they sat trapped as German forces closed in on them. In Britain, the May 10 invasion led Prime Minister Neville Chamberlain to resign, making way for a new government headed by Winston Churchill. A plan to evacuate the Allied troops from France was hatched, but time was running out.

Then help came from an unexpected source: On May 24, Adolf Hitler ordered German Panzers to stop their advance on Dunkirk.

The evacuation, code-named Operation Dynamo, began on May 26. The Royal Navy's large ships couldn't go near the shallow Dunkirk beach, so a call was put out for small craft to help. Before it was over, an armada of small boats,

The city of Rotterdam was in ruins after Germany's 1940 invasion of the Netherlands.

many of them leisure or fishing crafts, aided in the evacuation, which ended on June 4. Some 338,000 men were rescued.

Weeks later, on June 11, France formally surrendered to Germany. There would be no more fighting on the western front until the invasion of Normandy in 1944.

FINEST HOUR: BATTLE OF BRITAIN

On June 18, Winston Churchill told Britain's House of Commons that the Battle of France was over and the Battle of Britain was about to begin. (For more, see page 74.)

"Let us therefore brace ourselves to our duties," he said, "and so bear ourselves, that if the British Empire and its Commonwealth last for a thousand years, men will still say, 'This was their finest hour.'"

Hitler's planned invasion of Britain, called Operation Sea Lion, required Germany to first gain control of the skies over England and the English Channel. The air battle began on June 10, 1940, when the Luftwaffe attacked British coastal defenses and radar stations.

By mid-August, German aircraft, including Messerschmitt Bf-109 fighters, were taking on Royal Air Force Spitfire and Hawker Hurricane fighters in dogfights over England. Some Royal Air Force pilots scrambled more than five times a day to meet the attacks.

THE BLITZ

In late August, Luftwaffe bombers aiming for military targets drifted off course and dropped bombs on London. Britain retaliated by bombing Berlin. Enraged, Hitler

German infantrymen
operate near
Dunkirk, France,
in 1940.

English children sit amid the rubble of London during the Blitz.

ordered a full-scale bombing of London. The Blitz, as it came to be known, began on Sept. 7, 1940, and continued for months.

Hitler hoped to demoralize the British with the attacks, which caused enormous damage and killed more than 40,000 civilians. But he misjudged the dogged spirit with which Londoners met the bombing, and by focusing his rage on civilians rather than military targets, Hitler doomed Operation Sea Lion. With the Luftwaffe sustaining ever greater losses, he canceled invasion plans and looked eastward.

OPERATION BARBAROSSA

Hitler's invasion of the Soviet Union has been called his greatest blunder. But there was more than just faulty military judgment behind the ill-advised move. Hitler held that ethnic Russians were "born slaves who feel the need of a master." He also believed that the Soviet state was ready to collapse. "We have only to kick in the door and the whole rotten structure will come crashing down," he told his generals.

That appeared to be the case after the Nazis launched Operation Barbarossa on June 22, 1941,

sending some 3 million men, 3,000 tanks, 7,000 artillery pieces and 2,500 aircraft into Soviet territory along an 1,800-mile front from Norway to the Black Sea. Over the following month, German forces swept forward in three main thrusts, encircling and driving back disorganized Soviet armies.

By July the Germans were just 200 miles from Moscow. Micromanaging his armies, Hitler once again squandered the opportunity by shifting forces back and forth between a thrust at Moscow and a thrust into Ukraine, the Soviet breadbasket. As a result, neither achieved its objective before winter. With frostbite decimating ill-clad German troops and the icy temperatures paralyzing German tanks, Operation Barbarossa came to a halt.

THE BATTLE OF STALINGRAD

In the spring of 1942, Joseph Stalin and his generals expected a new German offensive against Moscow. Instead, the Germans decided to strike to the south and gain control of the oil fields of the Caucasus. Another objective of the southern thrust was Stalingrad, an industrial city on the Volga River. Hitler saw propaganda value in occupying a city named after the Soviet leader.

The battle for Stalingrad began in mid-August of 1942 and lasted a little more than five months. Assigned to take the city, the German 6th army met fierce resistance and was bogged down by room-by-room fighting. Stalin sent more troops to the city, and as fighting raged in the streets, he issued an order to Stalingrad's defenders: "Not a step back!"

Soviet generals Georgy Zhukov and Aleksandr Vasilevsky then organized Soviet troops near the city and launched a counterattack that encircled the Germans fighting inside Stalingrad. The Soviets kept tightening the noose as winter set in. By February 1943, Soviet troops had retaken the city, capturing 100,000 Axis troops, few of whom survived Russian prison camps.

THE STRATEGIC INITIATIVE SHIFTS

Three months after the German defeat at Stalingrad, Churchill boarded the S.S. *Queen Mary*, bound for the United States to discuss war strategy with

Trapped British troops are evacuated from Dunkirk during Operation Dynamo.

An aerial view of the bombing of London in 1940: Ultimately more than 40,000 civilians were killed.

President Franklin D. Roosevelt. The ship had been painted austere gray and stripped of its finery, but Churchill proudly pointed out that his lifeboat had been equipped with a machine gun.

The situation was very different now from what it had been when Churchill spent Christmas at the Roosevelt White House in December 1941, just after the Japanese surprise attack on Pearl Harbor. In the Atlantic, U-boats were being hunted down, thanks to British codebreakers. In the skies over Europe, U.S. Army Air Force B-17 bombers were pounding German industry. And in the Soviet Union, Stalin's Red Army had handed Hitler a crushing setback.

In May of 1943, as Churchill set out on his journey to the United States, he could also enjoy some other welcome news: the imminent collapse of Axis forces in North Africa.

VICTORY IN NORTH AFRICA

The British had been fighting in North Africa—first against Italian armies, then against German and Italian armies—since 1940. Battles had been lost and won for control of Egypt and Libya, but the most significant Allied win came with the Battle of El Alamein in Egypt.

There, in October 1942, British Gen. Bernard Montgomery handed German Gen. Erwin Rommel's Afrika Korps a stinging defeat, pushing it into Tunisia.

Then in November 1942, British and American forces had landed in Morocco and moved westward. In February 1943, Americans fighting in the Atlas Mountains of Tunisia were badly beaten in the Battle of Kasserine Pass, with a cost of 6,000 casualties. But the Allied armies went on to trap the Axis forces, which surrendered on May 13, 1943.

THE NEXT STEP: SICILY

In the Soviet Union, Stalin still faced most of the German war machine, and he prodded the U.S. and Britain to open a western front. Churchill preferred attacking Italy, calling it the "soft underbelly" of Europe. American generals thought operations in the Mediterranean would simply dissipate the forces needed for more vital objectives. But during his conference with Roosevelt in May 1943, Churchill's position prevailed.

The Allies first invaded Sicily in July 1943 with armies led by U.S. Gen. George Patton and Britian's Montgomery. The invasion sent shock waves through the Fascist Italian government, which booted Benito Mussolini out of office and imprisoned him. By Aug. 17, Allies marched into the Sicilian port city of Messina, only to find that some 100,000 German and Italian troops had escaped to the Italian mainland.

Londoners take shelter in an Underground station during the Blitz.

Soviet civilians were hanged by German soldiers during Operation Barbarossa in September 1941.

By February 1943, Soviet troops had retaken the city of Stalingrad.

ITALY: THE LONG, HARD SLOG

Allied forces invaded the Italian mainland in September 1943, and what followed was a grinding, brutal fight. Italy formally surrendered to the Allies on Sept. 3, but the German army rapidly moved in to take control.

Mussolini was freed and placed at the head of a puppet regime, while German Field Marshall Albert Kesselring set up strong defensive lines across the Italian boot, turning the Allied advance into a series of costly battles.

On June 5, 1944, U.S. Gen. Mark Clark's Fifth Army entered Rome. By then, though, Italy had become a far less important prize than imagined by Churchill: With Allied troops getting ready to storm the beaches of France, the armies in Italy were told to stop their advance and to try to pin down as many German troops as possible for the duration of the war.

German forces in Italy would finally surrender on May 2, 1945, two days after the collapse of Berlin. The Allies and the Germans each suffered more than 300,000 casualties fighting for Europe's soft underbelly.

OPERATION OVERLORD BEGINS

Over the last days of May 1944, Roosevelt kept up a show of routine work, but his secretary, Grace Tully, noticed that "every movement of his face and hands reflected the tightly contained state of his nerves."

The cause for the president's tension was Operation Overlord, the impending Allied invasion of France.

To lead the invasion, Roosevelt had chosen U.S. Gen. Dwight Eisenhower, who had proven himself as commander of the multinational operations in North Africa and Italy. As Supreme Allied Commander, Eisenhower oversaw months of planning for the D-Day invasion. A huge fleet of warships had been assembled to deliver 160,000 American, British and Canadian troops across a 50-mile

Winston Churchill (second from right) went to America to discuss strategy in May 1943.

stretch of heavily fortified coastline in Normandy, and a date had been set: June 5, one of a handful of days when necessary conditions—a late-rising moon for paratroopers and a low tide at dawn—were right.

As D-Day approached, Roosevelt and Eisenhower knew its success or failure, and the fate of the war, depended not on generals or presidents, but on the soldiers who would have to climb out of landing crafts into water that was often over their heads, and then onto beaches raked by ferocious German fire.

THE LONGEST DAY

The invasion of Normandy was ultimately rescheduled because of

British Gen. Bernard Montgomery (center) prepares for the Battle of El Alamein.

It took six days for Allied troops to secure the beaches after landing at Normandy.

Strong defenses and high early casualties made it difficult at first for Allied troops to advance on D-Day.

German paratroopers rescued and imprisoned Benito Mussolini in September 1943.

stormy weather and didn't begin until 6:30 a.m. on June 6. By that point, more than 20,000 airborne troops had been dropped behind enemy lines by parachute or glider, tasked with securing bridges and roads ahead of ground troops. Many paratroopers missed their designated landing sites and drowned in marshes that had been flooded by Nazi engineers. British and Canadian troops captured beaches code-named Gold, Juno and Sword.

Americans landed at Utah Beach and Omaha Beach, where the fighting was fiercest. High seas swamped boats, and landing craft were pushed off course. Disembarking out of position at Utah Beach, Brig. Gen. Theodore Roosevelt Jr., son of the former president, famously said, "We'll start the war from right here."

By day's end, however, the Allies had a foothold in France. The National D-Day Memorial Foundation has estimated that 4,414 Allied soldiers died on D-Day—2,501 of them Americans. (For more on D-Day, see page 82.) ⊕

AIR WAR
THE COSTLY SCHWEINFURT FACTORY RAIDS

The U.S. Army Air Corps' Eighth Air Force flew its first mission in Europe on Aug. 17, 1942, when 18 Boeing B-17 Flying Fortresses escorted by British Spitfire fighters successfully bombed rail yards in northern France. A year later, on Aug. 17, 1943, the Eighth Air Force launched Mission 84, a double strike by 376 B-17s against factories in Schweinfurt and Regensburg, Germany. Without escort fighters, the bombers were easy targets The Regensburg group lost 24 aircraft; the Schweinfurt 36 planes, and 564 men were killed or captured.

The bombers failed to knock out the Schweinfurt factory, so another mission was launched in October. Of the 291 B-17s on the raid, 60 were shot down and 650 of 2,900 crewmen were lost.

By war's end, the Eighth Air Force lost upwards of 26,000 men—more than all the U.S. Marines who were killed fighting in the Pacific.

British Hawker Hurricanes helped take down the Luftwaffe; the planes scored the highest number of Royal Air Force (RAF) victories during the Battle of Britain.

THE BATTLE OF BRITAIN

1940

ON THE GROUND, A CITY RINGED WITH FIRE.
ABOVE, A DUEL FOR AIR SUPREMACY.

IN MAY 1940, German armies smashed through the Netherlands and Belgium. They were led by fast-moving armored divisions that quickly staggered and split the British and French forces stationed in the area. Roughly 338,000 British army soldiers were trapped on the French coast near the small town of Dunkirk between May 26 and June 4 and had to be evacuated by sea, abandoning much of their armament. Hitler's troops entered Paris on June 14 and France surrendered on June 22, leaving a crippled Britain to fight on alone.

There was little doubt about what was coming next. "The Battle of France is over. I expect that the battle of Britain is about to begin," British Prime Minister Winston Churchill told Parliament on June 18, 1940. The German Luftwaffe soon began air raids from France in order to seize control of the skies over England prior to a full-scale invasion. The only thing that stood between survival and defeat for the British were Royal Air Force (RAF) pilots who raced into the skies to fend off the relentless attacks.

"The RAF, outnumbered four to one, proved itself plane for plane and man for man better than the Luftwaffe," noted the American historian Henry Steele Commager in his 1945 book *The Story of the Second World War*.

In his book, Commager included an account by an English flyer, 21-year-old Pilot Officer John Maurice Bentley Beard, who recalled the action that took place one particular day in the summer of 1940, after word arrived at his base near London that German attackers were making their way toward the city. Beard's squadron took off and climbed to 15,000 feet, where they began scanning the skies for the enemy. Soon they were in view.

"It was really a terrific sight and quite beautiful," Beard remembered later. "First they seemed just a cloud of light as the sun caught the many glistening chromium parts of their engines, their windshields, and the spin of their airscrew discs. Then, as our squadron hurtled nearer, the details stood out. I could see the bright-yellow noses of Messerschmitt fighters sandwiching the bombers, and could even pick out some of the types. The sky seemed full of them, packed in layers thousands of feet deep. They came on steadily, wavering up and down along the horizon. 'Oh, golly,' I thought, 'golly, golly....'"

THE MIGHTY LUFTWAFFE

After World War I, a defeated Germany was forbidden by the Treaty of Versailles to have an air force. But in 1935, two years after Adolf Hitler became Germany's chancellor, the Luftwaffe was created, and by the start of World War II it was the most powerful air force in the world. The Luftwaffe had played a crucial role in Germany's victorious blitzkrieg attacks across Poland, Belgium and France, and as Hitler eyed an invasion of Britain, he hoped its reputation would cower Britain into surrendering peacefully. But he vastly underestimated the will of the British people and their leader.

Britain's Royal Air Force had been desperately training pilots as war came to Europe—men like

While the Germans initially targeted airfields and aircraft factories, they soon switched to bombing London.

John Beard. Born in 1918, he had attended college and was working at a bank when he joined the Royal Air Force Voluntary Reserve in 1937. Beard received his wings shortly before the outbreak of the war, and by the summer of 1940 he was part of a squadron flying Hawker Hurricane fighters, which along with Supermarine Spitfires were the mainstays of Britain's defense.

The air battle began in July, when the Luftwaffe began targeting coastal defenses and ports in England. By mid-August, German Messerschmitt BF-109 fighters were attacking British airfields and other facilities. When the RAF retaliated by bombing Berlin, Hitler sent his bombers to London.

The attacks came day after day, and day after day the RAF pilots scrambled to fend them off. "Accounts of individual feats of heroism by RAF pilots are numberless," Commager wrote in his history of the war. John Beard recalled that any tension he had

as he entered the air battle over London soon left him. "I was elated but very calm," he noted. Once given the order to attack, Beard's squadron dived into the thick of the German planes.

"I took my hand from the throttle lever so as to get both hands on the stick, and my thumb played neatly across the gun button. You have to steady a fighter just as you have to steady a rifle," he remembered. Zeroing in on a German Heinkel 111 bomber, he fired. The Heinkel, he noted, "went down in a spin, blanketed with smoke and with pieces flying off." Then he saw another group of bombers, these protected by Messerschmitt fighters, and raced toward them. As he did so, a group of Spitfires zoomed past him and attacked the Germans. "They must have each got one, for an instant later I saw the most extraordinary sight of eight German bombers and fighters diving earthward together in flames," Beard remembered.

FINEST HOUR

Over the summer and fall of 1940, Britain's air defense was tested almost to its limit, but it would not break. With Luftwaffe losses mounting, Adolf Hitler decided to forgo an invasion of the country and instead turned his attention to planning an invasion of the Soviet Union. British Prime Minister Winston Churchill would later say of the RAF flyers' heroism, "Never before in human history was so much owed by so many to so few."

On Oct. 25, John Beard was shot down during a mission over England, but he managed to bail out of his fighter. He landed safely, though wounded. After recovering, he rejoined his squadron in January 1941. One source notes that Beard ended the war with seven confirmed air victories. According to another report, he later became involved in the furniture business before setting up his own electrical engineering company, as peace returned to the world. ⊕

"While not all victims were Jews, all Jews were victims," wrote famed Holocaust survivor Elie Wiesel.

SYSTEMATIC EVIL

THE NAZIS' DESPICABLE PLAN OF GENOCIDE
LED TO THE DEATH AND SUFFERING OF
MILLIONS THROUGHOUT EUROPE.

THE NAZIS HAD a term to classify people whose lives they considered unimportant and whose elimination would better society: Lebensunwertes Leben, or "life unworthy of life." The phrase was applied to the mentally impaired and later to those considered "sexually deviant" and "racially inferior," as well as anyone judged to be an enemy of the state. In the end, it led to abomination as rival groups in the Nazi Party and the German state competed to carry out what they believed to be Adolf Hitler's wishes.

From very early in the war, part of Nazi policy was to imprison and murder civilians en masse. In March 1933, soon after Hitler became chancellor, Germany erected its first concentration camps to hold political prisoners such as German Communists, Socialists and Social Democrats. Soon, Jehovah's Witnesses, Roma, homosexuals, and others deemed to be "asocials" also were imprisoned. The camps allowed the Nazis to both exploit forced labor and eliminate those they wished, away from public and judicial review. "Imprisonment in the Nazi concentration camps was usually indefinite, and whilst (initially) some people were released in just a few days, most endured weeks, months or years of detention," notes the Wiener Holocaust Library. "Sanitation and facilities were extremely poor across all camps. Brutal treatment, torture and humiliation was commonplace."

Two years later, the Nazi party enacted the Nuremberg Laws, defining Jews as "non-Aryans" and stripping German Jews of their citizenship. After Germany annexed Austria in March 1938, thousands of German and Austrian Jews were arrested and detained in the Dachau, Buchenwald and Sachsenhausen concentration camps. The mass detention of Jews intensified the following November, after the notorious Kristallnacht ("Night of the Broken Glass") pogrom, in which Nazis in Germany violently burned synagogues and

Children had one of the lowest rates of survival at the camps, but thousands were hidden or given false identities to avoid being sent away.

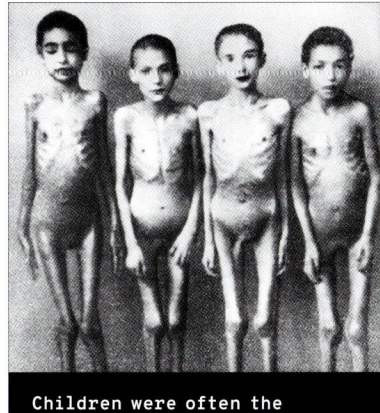

> "Justice for crimes against humanity must have no limitations."
> —Simon Wiesenthal

vandalized or destroyed Jewish homes and businesses.

But that was just the beginning. Germany's invasion of Poland in 1939 brought vast territorial conquests and many more potential prisoners, leading to the rapid expansion of the concentration camp system to the east. A policy of Jewish ghettoization, forced labor and systematic murder grew into the Nazi's "Final Solution": the elimination of Jews in Europe. As the Nazis made their way through Europe, new camps were quickly built. In December 1941, the Chelmno extermination camp near the Polish city of Łódź began its operations, becoming the first killing center to use poison gas to commit mass murder.

The following month, high-ranking Nazi Party and German government officials gathered

Children were often the subject of cruel experiments at Auschwitz.

in the Berlin suburb of Wannsee to coordinate plans for the extermination of European Jews. After the so-called Wannsee Conference, the Bełżec, Sobibór and Treblinka extermination camps were built in Poland, near railway lines to make transportation efficient.

In March 1942, the notorious Auschwitz-Birkenau camp, a combined concentration, forced labor and extermination camp, began operating in occupied Poland. It would soon become the deadliest of the camps: The Holocaust Memorial Museum estimates that of the 1.3 million people sent there, 1.1 million died, including 1 million Jews.

By 1945, the Allied armies had begun to liberate the concentration camps, where they discovered hundreds of thousands of starving and sick prisoners trapped with thousands of corpses, plus thousands of mass graves and high-volume crematoriums. By war's end, the Nazis had murdered more than 10 million people through the concentration camps, including 6 million Jews. ⊕

Nearly 7,000 naval vessels manned by nearly 200,000 sailors took part in the allied invasion of Normandy.

OMAHA BEACH

D-DAY

JUNE 6, 1944

CONFUSION, BRAVERY AND VICTORY RULED
THE DAY AS THE ALLIES LAUNCHED AN
ALL-OUT ASSAULT ON NAZI-HELD FRANCE.

THE ALLIED INVASION of Europe began in the early hours of June 6, 1944, when thousands of paratroopers from the American 82nd and 101st Airborne Divisions and the British 6th Airborne Division were dropped inland behind the German defenses along the Normandy coast of France. Their job was to take and hold key approaches to the Allied beachhead. A few hours later, aerial and naval bombardment opened up on German positions. And just after dawn, an armada of Allied ships began to disgorge the first troops assaulting a 50-mile stretch of coastline that had been divided into five sectors, code-named Utah, Omaha, Gold, Juno and Sword.

U.S. Army Lt. Robert Edlin, a rifle company platoon leader in Company A of the 2nd Ranger Battalion, was part of the first wave of troops to land on Omaha Beach, where the fighting that day would be the fiercest. Edlin had joined the Indiana National Guard at age 17 and gone to officer training school. He later volunteered for the Rangers, a light infantry force. Approaching Omaha Beach, his assault boat became mired on a sand bar some 75 yards from shore, so he and his men had to jump into the water and wade ashore.

Edlin would later recount his wartime experiences in journalist Gerald Astor's 1994 book *June 6, 1944: The Voices of D-Day.* He remembered the water off Omaha Beach as being miserably cold, and the bodies of American soldiers floating all around him. A nearby U.S. assault craft took a direct hit from a German battery. "I thought, there goes half of B Company."

Once on the beach, Edlin urged men pinned down by fire to move forward, but many didn't or couldn't—the preinvasion bombing had been ineffective in smashing German guns. Edlin was shot in both legs and, looking at the carnage around him, thought the invasion had been a failure. "We would be dead or prisoners soon," he assumed. "Everyone had withdrawn and left us." He learned otherwise when an Army colonel crawled over to him and said that the beach had been taken. "This colonel looked at me and said, 'You've done your job,'" Edlin recalled. "I answered, 'How? By using up two rounds of German ammo on my legs?'" Edlin was evacuated to England the following day and would later rejoin his unit as it battled through France.

OPENING A NEW FRONT

Preparations for the Allied invasion of Europe, code-named Operation Overlord, began in 1943. During the months leading up to the attack, the Allies carried out a complex deception plan, code-named Operation Bodyguard, to mislead German military planners as to the timing and place of the invasion. It worked: Hitler's armies, already stretched thin by having to defend the entire coast of northwest Europe, were taken by surprise when the Normandy landings began.

The Allies landed around 156,000 troops on D-Day, 73,000 of them American. They came ashore under withering fire from gun emplacements overlooking beaches that had been covered with wooden stakes, land mines, metal obstacles and barbed wire.

The operation had to take place in a small, three-day window based on changing tides and moonlight.

"The real hero is the man who fights even though he is scared," Gen. George Patton told his troops on June 5, before the invasion began.

It wasn't until June 11 that all the beaches were fully secured and more than 326,000 troops and 100,000 tons of equipment had landed at Normandy. Hitler, still believing the invasion was a feint designed to distract the Germans from a coming attack north of the Seine river, refused to release nearby divisions to join the counterattack. By the end of June, the Allies had seized the vital port of Cherbourg.

The National D-Day Memorial Foundation has estimated that 4,414 Allied soldiers died in the invasion, 2,501 of them Americans. Casualty figures are notoriously difficult to verify, but the accepted estimate is that the Allies suffered a total of 10,000 total casualties on D-Day itself. The highest casualties occurred on Omaha Beach, where 2,000 U.S. troops were killed, wounded or went missing. The vast majority of the men who died perished in the first waves of the attack. German casualties on D-Day have been estimated between 4,000 and 9,000 men.

WORDS OF COURAGE

The stories about what happened on D-Day have become legend— told in countless history books and memoirs (Edlin himself was the subject of a biography, *The Fool Lieutenant: A Personal Account of D-Day and World War II*), as well as in films such as *The Longest Day* and *Saving Private Ryan*. Another way of understanding what happened on the beaches of Normandy is through the letters that soldiers wrote to families back home. Some of them are collected in the 2001 book *War Letters: Extraordinary Correspondence from American Wars*, compiled by Andrew Carroll, including one from a 28-year-old Army staff sergeant, Eugene Lawton, who wrote to his parents in Tarentum, Pennsylvania.

"One's thoughts go deep into the past when moving across water on a

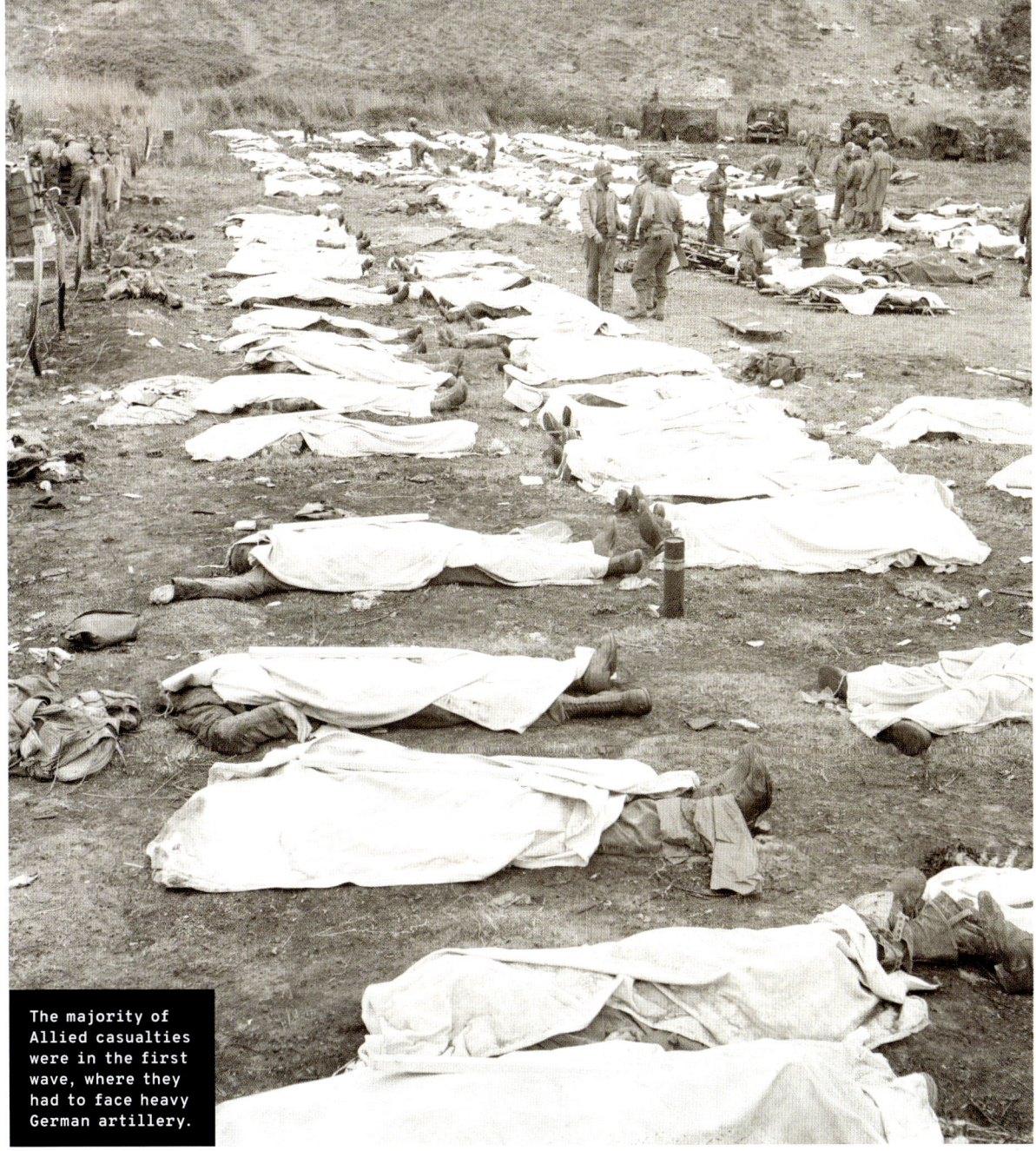

troop ship," he wrote. "And [I] can say the move to France left me with the feeling of 'seeing the past and trying to look through the fog into the future.'" Lawton went on to describe the confusion of the fighting that day. "Couldn't figure out where the enemy was that fired at us coming in on the beach," he recalled. "Later on in rear area [we] found out [it] was a sniper [who was] giving us trouble."

"Yes Mom and Dad," he concluded, "I have told you about a few things up to a certain point. Am afraid I can't go beyond what have already told you." Military censors prevented him from providing more precise information, he noted.

"Can say I was hit," he added, "but as to date, time, and place, well, as censorship doesn't permit it, why try to write about it?"

The letter, posted from England, where Lawton was recovering, was one of his last: He was killed months later in Belgium during the Battle of the Bulge. ✪

CHAPTER 3

THE PACIFIC THEATER

AFTER THE ATTACK ON PEARL HARBOR, THE U.S.
TURNED ITS ATTENTION TO THE FARAWAY EAST.

The U.S. aircraft carrier *Yorktown* listed and sank during the Battle of Midway, June 7, 1942.

WAR
ACROSS THE PACIFIC

KEY OFFENSIVE AND COUNTEROFFENSIVE
MOVES, FROM PEARL HARBOR TO
JAPAN'S FRONT LINE OF DEFENSE.

THE MAN WHO masterminded the Japanese attack on Pearl Harbor understood the likely consequences of a war with the United States. Adm. Isoroku Yamamoto, the chief of Japan's combined fleet, warned his government that while Japan's military could overrun weak Allied forces in the Pacific for up to one year, the U.S. would prevail in a prolonged war of attrition.

Yamamoto had seen the source of America's power—its industrial might—in person. While serving as a naval attaché in Washington, D.C., in the late 1920s, he'd toured the U.S. and marveled at its factories. In the 1930s Yamamoto, a political moderate, tangled with Japanese ultranationalists pushing for military aggression, and as naval vice minister he tried to stop Japan from forming an alliance with Nazi Germany and Fascist Italy. When it did so in 1940, the U.S. retaliated, as Yamamoto had predicted, by cutting off vital oil exports to the country. Its diplomatic options diminishing, Japan veered toward conflict, and Yamamoto, having failed to prevent a war, began preparing for it.

His plan, as historian Ian W. Toll has noted, would be an all-or-nothing gambit: "We should do our best to decide the fate of the war on the very first day," Yamamoto stated.

DAY OF INFAMY

The morning of Sunday, Dec. 7, 1941, was clear and bright in Honolulu—perfect conditions for the 353 Japanese aircraft arriving in waves to attack Pearl Harbor, home of the American Navy's Pacific Fleet since 1940. The planes, launched from six aircraft carriers, caught the U.S. military by surprise. The fleet's eight battleships were lost or severely damaged, while 2,403 people were killed—1,177 of them on the sunken battleship USS *Arizona*.

It was the worst disaster in U.S. naval history, but the damage could have been even greater: All the fleet's aircraft carriers happened to be elsewhere that day. (For more on Pearl Harbor, see page 102.)

President Franklin D. Roosevelt was in his White House study when he heard the news. As aides ran in and out of the room, Roosevelt sat at his desk with what his wife, Eleanor, called the "deadly calm" he often exhibited when hearing bad news.

Franklin D. Roosevelt delivers an altered speech to Congress following the Pearl Harbor attack.

The USS *Shaw*, an American destroyer, explodes during Japan's attack on Pearl Harbor.

And this was very bad, for it wasn't only Hawaii under attack. "Japan Strikes All Over Pacific," screamed the headline of the *Boston Daily Globe* on Dec. 8, the day Roosevelt addressed a joint session of Congress to ask for a declaration of war. His speech, as written, referred to Dec. 7, 1941, as "a date which will live in world history." Before delivering it, the president replaced "world history" with "infamy."

AGGRESSIVE MOVES

Japan swept across a vast front. The Philippine capital of Manila fell on Jan. 2, 1942, and on Jan. 7 Japanese forces attacked U.S. and Filipino military that had evacuated to Bataan in the Philippines. On Feb. 15, the British surrendered Singapore. On March 8, the Dutch surrendered Java. On March 11, Gen. Douglas MacArthur, commander of U.S. Army Forces in the Far East, left the Philippines and flew to Australia, where he was appointed commander of the Southwest Pacific Theater.

On April 9, Allied forces on Bataan surrendered, and 75,000 harshly treated prisoners were forced to walk in blazing heat toward a POW camp more than 60 miles away. Casualty estimates resulting from the so-called Bataan Death March vary greatly, from 5,000 to 18,000 Filipino deaths and 500 to 650 American deaths.

THE DOOLITTLE RAID

With American morale sagging from the onslaught of Japan's stunning victories, Roosevelt endorsed a risky air raid on Tokyo by a force of B-25 bombers under the command of Lt. Col. James Doolittle, a U.S. military aviation hero. On April 18, specially trained crews launched 16 of the bombers from the pitching deck of an aircraft carrier, the USS *Hornet*, some 650 miles from Japan. The bomber crews reached Tokyo shortly after noon, dropped their payloads and flew on to crash-land or parachute onto Chinese and Soviet territory. Of Doolittle's 80 crewmen, three died in a crash and eight were taken prisoner by Japan. Of those, four were killed in captivity.

While Doolittle's raid did little damage to Tokyo, it had an important unintended result. Alarmed Japanese leaders accepted a plan by Adm. Yamamoto intended to destroy the remainder of the U.S. Pacific Fleet, which he planned to do with a powerful naval attack on Midway Island, a U.S. outpost halfway between Japan and America.

BATTLE OF THE CORAL SEA

Japan also moved to strengthen its defense perimeter in the South Pacific by occupying Port Moresby in New Guinea. A fleet including two large aircraft carriers and a light carrier was sent to provide air cover for invasion forces, but plans for the attack were intercepted by the U.S. Navy, which sent two carriers and other ships to confront the Japanese.

What followed, on May 7 and 8, 1942, was the first battle between aircraft carriers. In the end, one Japanese light carrier was sunk and a larger fleet carrier suffered heavy damages, while the U.S. lost one carrier, the *Lexington*. Another carrier, the *Yorktown*, was severely crippled.

THE BATTLE OF MIDWAY

Yamamoto's plan for the battle of Midway Island included a diversionary attack on the Aleutian Islands near Alaska. An air attack on Midway itself would be launched from four Japanese aircraft carriers, the *Akagi*, *Kaga*, *Hiryu* and *Soryu*, commanded by Vice Adm. Chuichi Nagumo. When the U.S. Navy sent ships to reinforce

the island, Nagumo's carriers and a fleet led by Yamamoto himself would be waiting 600 miles to the west to pounce on them.

What Yamamoto didn't know was that the American Navy had broken the Japanese code, allowing Adm. Chester Nimitz, the U.S. Pacific Fleet commander, to set up a trap of his own. Yamamoto was also under the impression that the USS *Yorktown* had been sunk during the Battle of the Coral Sea. In fact, the carrier had limped to Pearl Harbor, where it was hastily repaired and then sent to join a U.S. force lying in wait for the Japanese fleet near Midway.

TURNING POINT

On June 4, Nagumo, as planned, launched an air strike against the island. His aircraft were refueling for a second attack when a Japanese scout plane spotted the American fleet east of Midway. Nagumo changed strategy, ordering his planes to prepare to attack the ships. Just then a wave of U.S. torpedo bombers from the carriers *Hornet* and *Enterprise* arrived to attack the Japanese ships. Nearly all were shot down by Japanese Zero fighters providing air cover for the fleet. But as the Zeros pursued the torpedo planes, U.S. dive bombers appeared and

"We haven't got the Navy to fight in both the Atlantic and the Pacific... so we will have to build up the Navy and the Air Force, and that will mean that we will have to take a good many defeats before we can have a victory."

—PRESIDENT FRANKLIN D. ROOSEVELT

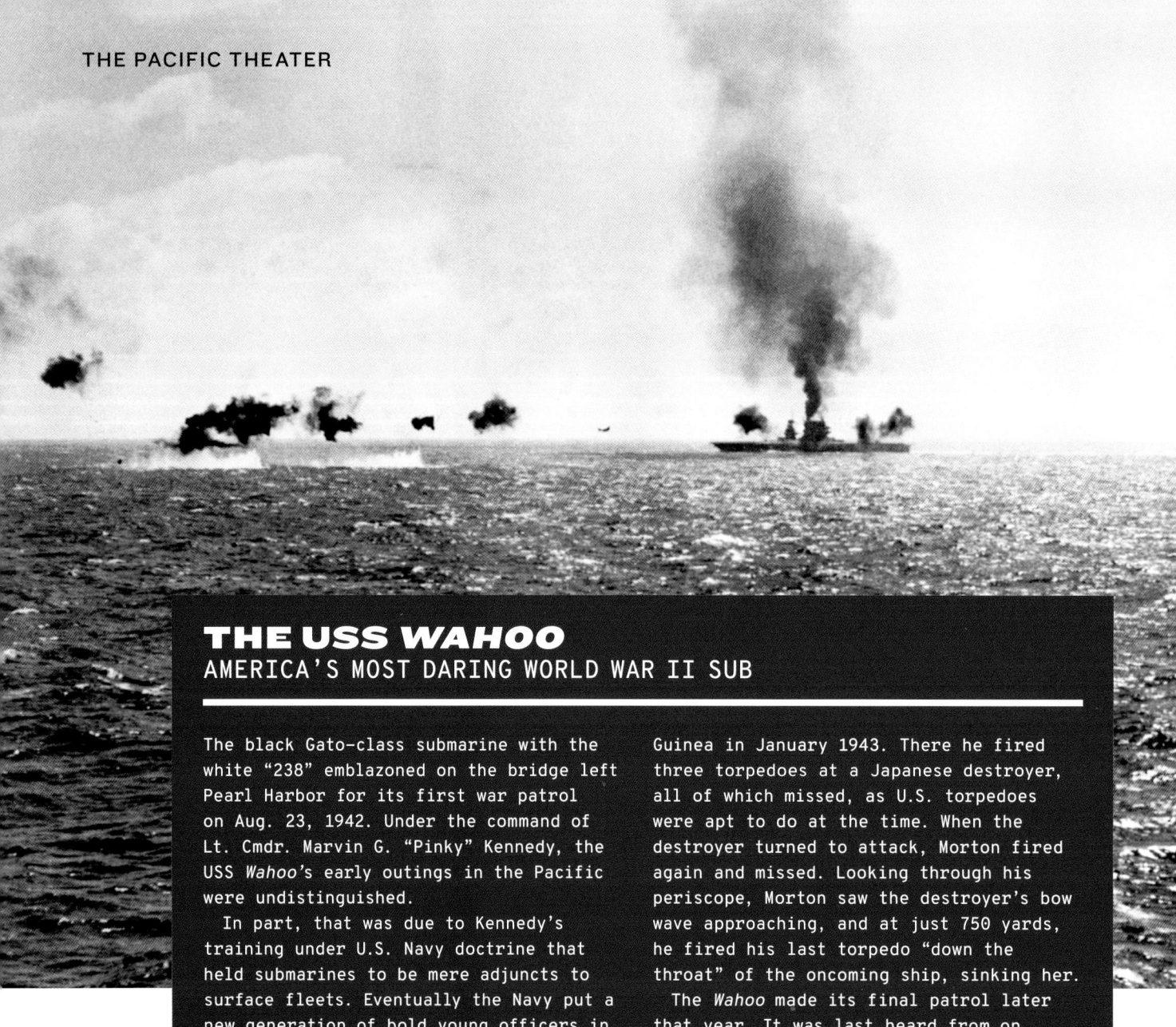

THE USS *WAHOO*
AMERICA'S MOST DARING WORLD WAR II SUB

The black Gato-class submarine with the white "238" emblazoned on the bridge left Pearl Harbor for its first war patrol on Aug. 23, 1942. Under the command of Lt. Cmdr. Marvin G. "Pinky" Kennedy, the USS *Wahoo*'s early outings in the Pacific were undistinguished.

In part, that was due to Kennedy's training under U.S. Navy doctrine that held submarines to be mere adjuncts to surface fleets. Eventually the Navy put a new generation of bold young officers in command of its submarines and sent them on long patrols to hunt Japanese naval and merchant shipping. At the end of 1942, Lt. Cmdr. Dudley Walker "Mush" Morton took command of the *Wahoo*. Under Morton, the submarine set a record for inflicting damage on the enemy.

In one daring feat, Morton took the *Wahoo* into a Japanese-held harbor in New Guinea in January 1943. There he fired three torpedoes at a Japanese destroyer, all of which missed, as U.S. torpedoes were apt to do at the time. When the destroyer turned to attack, Morton fired again and missed. Looking through his periscope, Morton saw the destroyer's bow wave approaching, and at just 750 yards, he fired his last torpedo "down the throat" of the oncoming ship, sinking her.

The *Wahoo* made its final patrol later that year. It was last heard from on Sept. 13, 1943, while headed to the Sea of Japan. Reports later suggested that it was sunk by Japanese aircraft in seas north of Japan. The sub's fate was not unusual: In all, 52 U.S. submarines were lost in World War II, along with some 3,500 crewmen—a mortality rate of 22%, higher than that of any branch of the armed services.

The USS *Lexington* is hit and burns during the Battle of the Coral Sea, May 8, 1942.

These B-25 bombers were on the USS *Hornet* prior to the Doolittle Raid.

attacked three Japanese carriers —the *Akagi*, *Kaga* and *Soryu*— setting them ablaze.

The Japanese carrier *Hiryu* launched attacks on the *Yorktown*, which had to be abandoned. Meanwhile, dive-bombers from all three American carriers returned to attack the *Hiryu*. By battle's end, all four Japanese carriers had been destroyed. On June 7 the wounded *Yorktown* listed to port and sank. (For more on the Battle of Midway, see page 108.)

THE BATTLE OF GUADALCANAL

With the decisive victory at Midway, the U.S. went on the offensive in the Pacific. In August 1942, American troops landed at Guadalcanal, one of the Solomon Islands in the South Pacific. They overwhelmed Japanese defenders and seized a vital airfield.

The Japanese wanted the island back, however. Guadalcanal became the site of a gruesome six-month fight that included seven major naval battles and almost continuous air combat. On land, Marines tenaciously held the airfield against Japanese counterattacks. By early February 1943, Japan had lost two-thirds of the 31,400 troops sent to fight on the island. The Marines and the Army had lost fewer than 2,000 soldiers. Japan also lost far more pilots, on top of its aviator losses at Midway. After Guadalcanal, Japan had little hope of resisting a counteroffensive.

YAMAMOTO'S FATE

By early February 1943, after the final evacuation of Japanese troops from Guadalcanal, Adm. Yamamoto must have known that Japan was headed for eventual defeat. He was fatalistic, telling colleagues that he did not expect to survive the war.

Once again, his prediction was right. In early April, Yamamoto flew to Rabaul on the island of New Britain in the Australian Territory of New Guinea, a stronghold seized by Japan in January 1942. On April 18 he was flying again, this time to tour front-line bases. Alerted by Navy codebreakers, 18 P-38 fighters dispatched from Guadalcanal shot down Yamamoto's plane near Bougainville in the Solomon Islands.

A TWO-FRONT STRATEGY

Now completely on the offensive, naval forces under the command of Adm. William "Bull" Halsey moved north through the Solomons, while troops under the command of Gen. Douglas MacArthur pushed along the northern coast of New Guinea, aiming, ultimately, at the Philippines. Here, an important decision was made: Rather than attack the powerful Japanese base at Rabaul, MacArthur's troops passed it by, striking instead at less defended islands to the west. Pinned down by Allied air and naval power, the large Japanese garrison at Rabaul was isolated and useless for the remainder of the war. The tactic, known as island-hopping, became a fixture of U.S. strategy in the Pacific.

At the same time, the United States launched a second front. While MacArthur went island-hopping across the South Pacific, the Navy began a campaign in the central Pacific with the invasion of Betio Island, part of the Tarawa atoll in the Gilbert Islands, in November 1943.

THE BATTLE OF TARAWA

The 18,000 Marines invading Betio on Nov. 20 expected to secure it easily. Instead, low tides made it impossible for some landing craft to clear the island's reef, and Japanese guns on the island opened fire on the stranded boats.

Defended by Japanese troops fighting from well-designed fortifications, the island became a killing ground. A Japanese admiral reportedly said that a million men could not take Tarawa in a hundred years. Instead it took three days, with the cost of some 1,000 American lives. Nearly the entire Japanese garrison, more than 4,000 troops and laborers, were killed.

COUNTEROFFENSIVE SURGE

By the end of 1943, Japanese air power in the Pacific had been greatly diminished, while the United States was putting to sea huge new fleets. On Jan. 31, 1944, U.S. troops supported by just such an armada invaded the Marshall Islands in the central Pacific.

Using lessons learned from the fighting on Tarawa, the U.S. overwhelmed the Japanese forces on Kwajalein Atoll in three days. Of 3,500 Japanese defenders, only 51 survived. With the victory, Adm. Nimitz decided the next target would be far to the east, at Japan's front line of defense.

Lt. Robert Hite was one of eight Doolittle Raid crewmen captured by the Japanese.

KILL THE BASTARDS!
DOWN THIS ROAD MARCHED ONE OF THE REGIMENTS
OF THE UNITED STATES ARMY
KNIGHTS SERVING THE QUEEN
OF BATTLES
TWENTY OF THEIR WOUNDED IN LITTERS WERE
BAYONETED, SHOT AND CLUBBED
BY THE YELLOW BELLIES
KILL THE BASTARDS!

This sign appeared on Guadalcanal after the six-month battle for the island ended in February 1943.

Marines navigate a sodden Guadalcanal after a rainstorm.

OPERATION FORAGER

Japanese military planning focused on the idea of a decisive naval battle that would destroy the U.S. fleet—much as Yamamoto had attempted in his failed move against Midway Island. Such was the hope of the Japanese Imperial Navy when the U.S. began its invasion of the Mariana Islands in June 1944.

The lure of those islands—Saipan, Guam and Tinian—was great for Nimitz: Just 1,300 miles southeast of Tokyo, they would become the base from which the U.S. could send its new B-29 Superfortress bombers to attack the Japanese home islands.

The invasion of the Marianas, called Operation Forager, began on the morning of June 15, just days after the D-Day invasion of France. At 7 a.m., American troops began riding landing craft toward the beaches of Saipan, launching what would become a bloody three-week-long struggle.

BATTLE BY LAND AND SEA

Preinvasion pounding of key targets by battleships and aircraft had missed many gun emplacements along cliffs overlooking Saipan's beaches, and U.S. troops faced concentrated fire during their landings, suffering more than 2,000 casualties. By the end of the day, however, 20,000 troops made it ashore and were ready to move into Saipan's landscape of jagged mountains and deep ravines.

Japanese prisoners from the Battle of Tarawa are pictured in November 1943.

"The sky at times was brighter than noontime on the equator. The arching, glowing cinders that were high-explosive shells sailed through the air as though buckshot were being fired out of many shotguns from all sides of the island."

—JOURNALIST ROBERT SHERROD, TARAWA

Meanwhile, with a huge U.S. fleet stationed in the Marianas in support of the troops, the Japanese navy saw its chance for a conclusive naval confrontation. The result was the Battle of the Philippine Sea on June 19 and 20—the largest battle between aircraft carrier forces in history. It was a defeat from which Japan's navy would never recover.

More than 3,000 American troops were killed and over 13,000 were wounded taking Saipan. Hopelessly trapped on the island, an estimated 27,000 Japanese soldiers died in its defense. Gen. Yoshitsugu Saito, commander of Japan's forces on Saipan, apologized to Tokyo for the defeat and committed ritual suicide, while in Japan Prime Minister Hideki Tojo was forced to resign.

By August, U.S. forces had taken the other Mariana Islands. A year later, a B-29 would take off from an airfield on Tinian loaded with an atomic bomb. Its destination: the Japanese city of Hiroshima. ✦

Nineteen U.S. Navy ships (including the USS *Maryland*, shown here) were destroyed in the deadly raid.

PEARL HARBOR

DECEMBER 7, 1941

THE NATION REACTED WITH SHOCK AS THE
U.S. SUDDENLY ENTERED WORLD WAR II.

CPL. E.C. NIGHTINGALE, a Marine aboard the USS *Arizona*, was just finishing his breakfast on Dec. 7, 1941—a sunny Sunday morning—when the battleship's siren for air defense first sounded. He paid little attention to it, but soon heard a nearby explosion. Moving toward a hatchway, he saw a bomb strike a barge floating alongside the neighboring battleship the USS *Nevada*, followed by machine gun fire. His ship's antiaircraft battery opened up and Nightingale began making his way toward his battle station. America was being attacked.

"I reached the boat deck and our antiaircraft guns were in full action, firing very rapidly," he recalled later in an account collected by the usarizona.org, an online repository of facts and stories relating to the attack on the U.S. naval base at Pearl Harbor on the island of Oahu, Hawaii. "I was about three-quarters of the way to the first platform on the mast when it seemed as though a bomb struck our quarterdeck. I could hear shrapnel or fragments whistling past me."

USS *Arizona* Ensign Guy S. Flanagan was in his bunk when he heard the air raid siren. "Then I heard the explosion. I was undressed. I climbed into some khaki clothes and shoes," he noted in an account at usarizona.org. At first, Flanagan thought it was all some kind of joke. Gunner's Mate (GM) Second Class Donald Eugene Gordon heard the siren and went to his battle station. "We started to get the guns ready for firing while being tossed around by bombs hitting the ship," he recalled. "There was a big explosion and the ship raised up and settled down. The last man to leave the handling room was knee-deep in water. He climbed straight up three decks to the gun pits and was still knee-deep in water."

Ten minutes after Japanese aircraft first appeared over Pearl Harbor, home of the U.S. Navy's Pacific Fleet, a bomb crashed through the *Arizona*'s armored decks and detonated in the ship's ammunition magazine. Nightingale, Flanagan and Gordon all lived through the day, but they were among the lucky ones. By the time the attack was over, 1,177 *Arizona* crewmen were dead; only 333 survived. Eight U.S. Navy battleships were sunk or severely damaged, along with other ships. In all, 2,403 Americans were killed during the attack.

WARNINGS OF DANGER

The U.S. Pacific Fleet had been stationed at Pearl Harbor since April 1940, a time during which tensions were rising between the United States and the Empire of Japan. In the summer of 1940, the U.S. began to restrict the export of materials to Japan that could be used to fuel its aggression in China and elsewhere in the Pacific. As the possibility of war mounted, Adm. Husband E. Kimmel and Lt. Gen. Walter C. Short, who shared command at Pearl Harbor, had been advised of a possible attack. The most recent warnings had come on Nov. 24 and 27.

But response to the warnings proved to be highly inadequate. Short issued an order to be on alert for possible sabotage and

The Japanese battleship *Nagato* was the flagship of its fleet and where Adm. Isoroku Yamamoto oversaw the Pearl Harbor incursion.

An aerial view of Pearl Harbor prior to the attack. Ford Island is in the center; Hickam Field is in the upper left.

Honolulu Star-Bulletin 1st EXTRA

WAR!
OAHU BOMBED BY JAPANESE PLANES

SAN FRANCISCO, Dec. 7.—President Roosevelt announced this morning that Japanese planes had attacked Manila and Pearl Harbor.

SIX KNOWN DEAD, 21 INJURED, AT EMERGENCY HOSPITAL

concentrated fighter planes at Wheeler Field near Honolulu. He also ordered mobile radar units to begin scanning the area during nighttime hours, when an attack was expected to come.

A MORNING RAID

Instead, Japanese aircraft appeared over Pearl Harbor at 7:55 a.m. The planes—including fighters, dive bombers and torpedo bombers—had been launched from an Imperial Navy strike force of six aircraft carriers some 230 miles off the Hawaiian island of Oahu. Leading

the attack, aviator Capt. Mitsuo Fuchida sent the coded message "Tora Tora Tora" to the Japanese fleet to indicate the Americans had been caught by surprise.

Arriving in two waves, 353 aircraft joined in the attack over the 75 minutes. Japanese strafing destroyed U.S. aircraft packed tightly together on the ground. Along Pearl Harbor's Battleship Row, most of the damage was done in the first 30 minutes of the attack. The USS *Arizona* exploded and sank, as did the USS *West Virginia*. After being hit by four torpedoes in five minutes,

the USS *Oklahoma* rolled over. Sailors were ordered to abandon the USS *California* before it sank. The USS *Nevada* was making its way out of the harbor when the second wave of attackers arrived. Struck by a torpedo and at least six bombs, the

Soon after the bombings, President Franklin D. Roosevelt wrote an address asking Congress to declare war against Japan. His hope was to rally the nation together. Shown: A crowd gathers in New York after the Dec. 7 attack.

ship was grounded on a coral ledge. (It was later salvaged and put back into service.)

USS *West Virginia* gunner's mate Jim Downing and his wife were hosting breakfast for eight of his shipmates that morning when an anti-aircraft shell landed in their backyard. The radio announced the enemy attack and the men immediately jumped in a truck headed for Pearl Harbor, about 20 minutes away. By the time Downing made it to the *West Virginia*, the ship had already been hit by nine torpedoes. In 2015, Downing described that day to a San Diego television station:

"The saddest thing I saw that morning was sailors being blown off the ship, come up out of the water, feel the oil on their bodies... and they just became human torches," he said. "Once the Japanese had sunk our ship they didn't care, so all we had to do was fight the fires and take care of the wounded."

Japanese losses during the attack were light—various accounts estimate that at least 29 and as many as 60 planes were shot down and that fewer than 100 men were killed. For the shocked United States, there was one piece of good news: None of the fleet's aircraft carriers were in Pearl Harbor on Dec. 7. The following day, the United States officially declared war on Japan. ⊕

Griffith Baily Coale worked as a combat artist and captured the U.S. air attack on the Japanese aircraft carrier Kaga.

CLOSE-UP

THE BATTLE OF MIDWAY

JUNE 4, 1942

THE FIERY FIGHT IN THE PACIFIC HELPED
TURN THE TIDE OF THE WAR.

FOLLOWING JAPAN'S SWEEPING Pacific victories in late 1941 and early 1942, the U.S. struck back. On April 18, 1942, Lt. Col. James Doolittle led an air raid on Tokyo that did relatively little damage but, as it turned out, nonetheless helped change the course of the war.

The Japanese military had assumed the country's homeland was safe from attack. With that perception shattered after the air raid on Tokyo, Adm. Isoroku Yamamoto devised a plan to extend Japan's defensive perimeter by attacking Midway Island, a U.S. outpost a thousand miles from Hawaii. Yamamoto hoped the attack would lure the U.S. into a trap; he sent a powerful armada that included four fleet aircraft carriers toward Midway, anticipating a decisive battle for control of the Pacific. But the U.S., which had cracked the Japanese code and knew an attack was coming, laid a trap of its own, sending three of its aircraft carriers—the *Hornet*, *Enterprise* and *Yorktown*—to lay in wait off Midway.

On June 4, the Japanese struck, bombing Midway. U.S. planes soon discovered the Japanese fleet northeast of Midway, and at mid-morning, low-flying American torpedo bombers attacked the Japanese aircraft carriers. Japanese Zero fighters flying cover overhead dropped down to sea level and fired on the U.S. planes. On board one of the Japanese carriers, the *Akagi*, was Capt. Mitsuo Fuchida, the

Adm. Isoroku Yamamoto commanded the Japanese navy's Combined Fleet.

aviator who had led Japan's attack on Pearl Harbor six months earlier. Fuchida, who had recently had an emergency appendectomy and was unable to fly, was standing on the ship's bridge, where he witnessed the American attack. He would later recall what he saw in a book he wrote, *Midway: The Battle That Doomed Japan, The Japanese Navy's Story*.

"The distant wings flashed in the sun. Occasionally one of the specks burst into a spark of flame and trailed black smoke as it fell into the water," he remembered. "Our fighters were on the job. Presently, a report came in from a Zero group leader: 'All 15 enemy torpedo bombers shot down.'"

Soon another wave of torpedo bombers appeared, aiming straight for the *Akagi*. But these raiders, too, came without escorting fighters and were easy prey for the Japanese Zeros. One by one the American planes went into the sea, to the cheering of Japanese sailors.

Lt. Col. James Doolittle led the first U.S. aerial raid on Japan; after bailing out of his plane, he landed in a rice paddy in China.

Pictured: Artist rendering of a Japanese aircraft carrier being hit by American planes.

THE TIDE TURNS

With the American torpedo bombers destroyed, the Japanese soon prepared to launch another attack on Midway Island. But when Japanese scouting planes sighted the American fleet, the order was given instead to prepare for an attack on the U.S. ships. This meant having to refit the aircraft with torpedoes. At the same time, the Zero fighters normally safeguarding Japan's fleet from high above had returned to their carriers for refueling. At that crucial moment, American Douglas Dauntless dive bombers appeared in the unprotected skies overhead.

"I looked up to see three black enemy planes plummeting toward our ship," Fuchida would remember. "Some of our machine guns managed to fire a few frantic bursts at them, but it was too late."

An artist's rendering of the battle from above; as a result of the loss, Japan abandoned its plan to expand its reach in the Pacific.

In 1942, the Douglas Dauntless was a newcomer to the U.S. Navy and largely untested in battle, but the aircraft quickly proved its worth in the Battle of Midway. Screaming down from 20,000 feet, dive bomber pilots could essentially "aim" at targets by flying directly at ships and releasing their bombs at very low altitudes. On the *Akagi*, Fuchida instinctively fell to the deck as the American planes plunged toward his ship. Seconds later, blasts shook him. Then followed a startling quiet as the barking of guns suddenly ceased. "I got up and looked at the sky," Fuchida recalled. "The enemy planes were already gone from sight."

TURNING POINT

Looking around at the *Akagi*, Fuchida saw a hole in the flight deck, planes upended and spewing flame and black smoke. "Reluctant tears streamed down my cheeks as I watched the fires spread," he later wrote in his book.

In the aftermath of the American attack, three Japanese carriers—the *Akagi*, the *Kaga* and the *Soryu*—were ablaze. Japan's surviving carrier, the *Hiryu*, launched two waves of attacks on the USS *Yorktown*. The American carrier was hit and had to be abandoned, though it remained afloat. Dive bombers from all three U.S. carriers

Capt. Mitsuo Fuchida
(above, in 1961;
right, in 1941)
witnessed the attack
at Midway firsthand;
he was instrumental in
launching Japan's own
attack on Pearl Harbor
six months earlier.

returned to attack the *Hiryu*, setting it ablaze, too.

On June 6, Yamamoto ordered his ships to retreat. During the Battle of Midway, Japan lost four aircraft carriers, 300 aircraft and as many as 3,000 men, including more than 200 of its most experienced pilots. The U.S. lost a destroyer, the USS *Hammann*, and the abandoned *Yorktown*, which was finally sunk by a Japanese submarine on June 6. Some 360 U.S. servicemen were lost during the battle.

A SURVIVOR'S STORY

After the battle, Japan went on the defensive. While U.S. industry began to turn out bigger aircraft carriers and better aircraft, Japan could not replace its losses from Midway.

Capt. Mitsuo Fuchida survived the battle and went on to serve as a naval staff officer. On Aug. 5, 1945, he was attending a military conference with Japanese army officers in the city of Hiroshima when he received a telephone call from naval headquarters requiring him to return to Tokyo immediately.

The following day, a U.S. Army Air Force B-29 Superfortress dropped a 9,700-pound uranium-235 bomb on Hiroshima, destroying the city.

The day after the bombing, Fuchida and a small military group were sent to Hiroshima to assess the damage. It has been reported that everyone in the party later died of radiation poisoning—except Fuchida. After the war he became a widely traveled Christian evangelist. He settled permanently in the United States, although he never became a U.S. citizen. ⊕

CHAPTER 4

LIFE AT WAR

WHILE THE MAINLAND WAS NEVER UNDER ATTACK, AMERICANS
HUNKERED DOWN TO SUPPORT THE TROOPS ABROAD.

Men in Winston–Salem, North Carolina, line up to register for the draft in 1940.

A NATION
TRANSFORMED

WWII CHANGED THE WAY PEOPLE DRESSED,
ATE, WORKED AND PLAYED—AND
A POWERFUL NEW AMERICA WAS BORN.

President Franklin D. Roosevelt enacted the military draft even before Pearl Harbor.

WORLD WAR II brought Americans a new vocabulary. People shopped with "ration stamps" as foods like sugar, meat and coffee became scarce. Many grew "victory gardens" in backyards, vacant lots and public parks, then turned to "victory cookbooks" for recipes that made the most of rationed goods.

There were "scrap drives" to collect metal objects that could be recycled for military use. With nylon going to make parachutes, women donned "leg makeup"—tan-colored cosmetics with an eyebrow-penciled seam line.

Pamphlets and magazine articles helped aviation enthusiasts identify both foreign and U.S.-made aircraft flying overhead, giving rise to a popular pastime known as "plane spotting." Soldiers and civilians alike became familiar with the all-terrain general purpose vehicle, or GP, but it was simply called the "jeep." And while today we have email, during the war there was "V-mail" for corresponding with soldiers abroad. People wrote on special forms, and their letters—subject to military censorship—were copied to microfilm, sent away and then printed back on paper once they reached their destinations.

The new terms reflected just how quickly and profoundly the country changed during World War II. Those changes, large and small, would help usher in today's world.

YOU'RE IN THE ARMY NOW

By the summer of 1940, with Nazi Germany marching into France and Great Britain under the threat of invasion, Americans who once wanted their country to stay out of the war were beginning to take the Nazi threat seriously. In a poll done for *Life* magazine in July 1940, 71% of respondents supported "the immediate adoption of compulsory military training for all young men."

That September, Congress approved the nation's first peacetime military draft, creating a giant shift in American society. The 1940 selective service law required all men 21 to 45 years old to register with local draft boards. Those selected from a draft lottery were required to serve at least one year in the armed forces. Once the U.S. entered World War II, draft terms extended through the duration of the fighting.

By the end of the war in 1945, 50 million men between 18 and 45 had registered for the draft and 10 million had been inducted in the military, notes the National WWII Museum. Altogether, 16 million Americans served in the military during the war.

OUTPRODUCING THE ENEMY

The growing military needed firepower. A month after Pearl Harbor, President Franklin D. Roosevelt told Americans that "powerful enemies must be outfought and outproduced," and as the country rallied to the cause, industry was transformed. Automakers were at the forefront. Chrysler made airplane fuselages. General Motors made trucks and tanks. Packard made engines for the British Royal Air Force's Spitfire fighter. And Ford turned out one B-24 Liberator long-range bomber every 63 minutes.

In 1944 alone, noted filmmaker Ken Burns in his 2007 documentary *The War*, the United States built more planes than the Japanese did from 1939 to 1945, while shipyards turned out more tonnage in 1941 than Japan did in the entire war.

With factories running at full speed and millions of men away in the military, America quickly faced a labor shortage. That drove up wages, and millions of people from all over America relocated to take the well-paying jobs. Many

The Selective Training and Service Act of 1940 was the first peacetime draft in U.S. history.

of them were women, who now found job opportunities that had previously been denied to them. More than 310,000 women worked in the U.S. aircraft industry in 1943, representing 65% of the industry's total workforce.

One of the women who went to work was Rosalind P. Walter, who grew up in a wealthy New York family but spent her nights driving rivets into the metal bodies of Corsair fighter planes in a Connecticut aircraft plant. A newspaper wrote about Walter, and the story inspired songwriters Redd Evans and John Jacob Loeb to pen a popular tune called "Rosie the Riveter."

"All the day long whether rain or shine, she's a part of the assembly line," went the lyrics.

The song, in turn, inspired artist Norman Rockwell to create a cover illustration for the May 29, 1943, issue of the *Saturday Evening Post* depicting a muscular woman in overalls with a rivet gun in her

"**All the day long whether rain or shine, she's a part of the assembly line. She's making history, working for victory— Rosie, brrrrr, the Riveter. Keeps a sharp lookout for sabotage, sitting up there on the fuselage.**"

—"ROSIE THE RIVETER" SONG

The iconic "Rosie the Riveter" poster was created to boost morale among defense-plant workers in the war.

A female employee works at an aircraft plant in Fort Worth, Texas, in 1942.

EXECUTIVE ORDER 9066
INTERNING JAPANESE AMERICANS

After Pearl Harbor, fears of a Japanese attack on the U.S. mainland and false rumors about saboteurs at home prompted President Franklin D. Roosevelt to sign Executive Order 9066, which authorized the removal of resident enemy aliens from areas of the United States loosely identified as military zones.

The order, signed on Feb. 19, 1942, wasn't targeted at any specific group, but it fed into long-standing racism against Japanese Americans on the West Coast. Lt. Gen. John L. DeWitt, commander of the U.S. Army Western Defense Command, ordered the internment of 110,000 Americans of Japanese ancestry, both citizens and noncitizens of the U.S. Removed from their homes and businesses on short notice, they were sent to remote camps in Western states.

"If Roosevelt shrewdly understood the strength of America's democracy, he failed miserably to guard against democracy's weakness—the tyranny of an aroused public opinion," notes historian Doris Kearns Goodwin. Grimly focused on the war, Roosevelt was willing to forsake the civil rights of Japanese Americans.

One person in the White House who strongly opposed the order was Roosevelt's wife, Eleanor, who in 1943 visited the Gila River internment camp in Arizona. "These people were not convicted of any crime," she wrote years later, "but emotions ran too high, too many people wanted to wreak vengeance on Oriental looking people."

In 1944, a Supreme Court ruling halted the detention of U.S. citizens without cause. In 1988, President Ronald Reagan ordered that reparations be paid to former internment camp detainees or their descendants.

U.S. dominance in plane manufacturing helped win the war.

lap and a copy of Adolf Hitler's *Mein Kampf* under her foot. (The name "Rosie" can be seen on her lunch box.) Rockwell's model was a Vermont woman, Mary Doyle Keefe, who died in 2015.

Before Rockwell painted his Rosie, however, a Pittsburgh commercial artist named J. Howard Miller created a wartime poster that has since become iconic. Miller's poster was originally displayed in Westinghouse Electric Corp. plants in 1943 as a morale builder. His model wore a red polka-dot bandanna and flexed her arm, while the poster declared, "We can do it!" In the 1980s, Miller's poster was transformed into a feminist symbol, and the woman in it came to be known as Rosie the Riveter.

Miller's illustration was inspired by a photo agency image of a young woman working at an industrial lathe. Over the years a number of women stepped forward claiming to have been the worker in the picture, but the likeliest Rosie, according to recent research, was Naomi Parker Fraley, who as a 20-year-old worked at the Naval Air Station in Alameda, California. Fraley died in 2018 at age 96. Rosalind Walter, the original Rosie, died in March 2020 at age 95.

THE RATIONING BOOK

The war created shortages of rubber, metal, fabric for clothing, gasoline, tires and other goods, including food, all of which were earmarked for the military. Scarcities prompted the federal Office of Price Administration to create a complicated system of rationing. Every American was entitled to war-ration books filled with stamps that could be used to buy restricted items like sugar, coffee, meat and cheese.

The government encouraged people to make up for food shortages by growing victory gardens. By 1944, there were some 20 million of these gardens in the U.S., producing roughly 8 million tons of food—the equivalent of more than 40% of all the fresh fruits and vegetables consumed in the nation.

AFRICAN AMERICANS: FIGHTING FOR VICTORY AND EQUALITY

Of the 16 million U.S. soldiers in World War II, about 1 million were African Americans. Some 125,000 African American troops served overseas in segregated units, among them the celebrated Tuskegee Airmen, the first Black military aviators in the U.S. Army Air Corps. Trained at the Tuskegee Army Air Field in Alabama, the unit flew more than 15,000 missions in Europe and North Africa and earned more than 150 Distinguished Flying Crosses.

When the soldiers came home in 1945, it was to a country in which Blacks were still denied their civil rights under Jim Crow laws. But the war had brought important changes to American society. In 1940, nearly three-quarters of African Americans lived in Southern states, most in rural areas. With the war, millions relocated to cities in Northern and Western states and manufacturing boomtowns in search of jobs and social equality. Racial tensions rose in many places; in 1943, race riots broke out in Detroit, New York and several other cities.

In 1941, Black labor leader A. Philip Randolph, head of the

RECIPE FOR A ONE-EGG VICTORY CAKE

WITH WARTIME RATIONING, COOKS GOT PLENTY OF ADVICE ON HOW TO MAKE DO. THIS VINTAGE RECIPE CAME FROM THE *ROYAL BAKING POWDER COOKBOOK*

SERVING SIZE
Makes one 8-inch or one 2-layer cake.

INGREDIENTS
- ½ cup shortening
- ⅝ cup sugar
- 1 egg, well beaten
- ½ teaspoon vanilla extract
- ⅓ cup light corn syrup
- 1 cup milk
- 2 cups cake flower
- 2½ teaspoons Royal Baking Powder
- ¼ teaspoon salt

INSTRUCTIONS
1 Cream shortening well; add sugar slowly, beating in well.
2 Add beaten egg and vanilla; beat until well blended.
3 Blend syrup and milk.
4 Sift together dry ingredients and add alternately with liquid to first mixture.
5 Bake in 1 greased square pan (8 x 8 x 2 inches) in moderate oven at 350°F about 1 hour or in 2 greased 8-inch layer cake pans at the same temperature for about 30 minutes.
Note: Honey may be substituted for light corn syrup.

> **"Plan your victory garden now. Get your garden plot lined up. Get the advice of a garden expert if you need it. And be prepared to grow your own for victory."**
>
> —FROM *DIG FOR VICTORY*, A 1943 NEWSREEL

Brotherhood of Sleeping Car Porters, called for a march on Washington to challenge racial discrimination at defense plants. As a result, President Roosevelt issued Executive Order 8802 banning such discrimination.

In 1942, Black newspapers in America launched the "Double V" campaign, which stood for victory in the war abroad and victory over discrimination at home. It spotlighted the efforts of African American soldiers and workers in the war effort and helped redefine the idea of Black citizenship. In 1948, President Harry Truman issued an order desegregating the U.S. military.

CALL OF DUTY: THE ART OF PATRIOTISM

Nearly every aspect of American culture was touched by the war effort—including advertising, which adopted patriotic themes to sell products that often weren't available to consumers. "The tire crisis is still acute, of course, and you must conserve the tires you have," read a 1944 General Tire advertisement.

That was just one aspect of an immense public relations effort by the government, and private companies working closely with the government, to promote the idea that war was not just necessary, but morally right. In 1942, Roosevelt created the Office of War Information to disseminate propaganda through films, radio programs and magazines. Ad campaigns pitched everything from war bonds and factory work to carpooling.

The government also held competitions for artists to create patriotic posters that were hung in public areas. Some posters warned Americans about the danger of foreign spies, while others tapped into darker themes, presenting bloodthirsty Nazis and racist images of Japanese people. (For more on wartime art and propaganda, see page 126.) Today these campaigns offer a glimpse into the mood of a nation committed to an all-out war. ◉

African American Air Corps students learn Morse Code in World War II.

Tuskegee Airmen pose at Tuskegee Army Flying School in Alabama in 1942.

The Tuskegee Airmen shot down three German jets in a single day of fighting on March 24, 1944.

Masculine strength was a common theme in many wartime posters, where muscle-bound men were often pictured against the backdrop of mighty machines.

THE
ART
OF BATTLE

CREATED AS PART OF A WIDE-RANGING
GOVERNMENT PROPAGANDA EFFORT,
WORLD WAR II POSTERS HELPED
PERSUADE AMERICANS TO DO WHATEVER
IT TOOK TO ACHIEVE VICTORY.

AMERICA NEEDED MORE than rifles, tanks, airplanes and ships to fight the war. The country had to mobilize not only an army, but also a civilian population that would be called upon to make sacrifices large and small before victory could be declared.

When Britain and France went to war with Germany in 1939, Americans were very much divided over whether the country should join the fight against fascism. While isolationists preached the danger of foreign entanglements and promoted an "America first" policy, President Franklin D. Roosevelt moved to support countries trying to hold Hitler at bay, at the same time promising

that he wouldn't send American boys into battle. The public's feelings changed dramatically when the Japanese attacked Pearl Harbor in December of 1941. After America entered the war in Europe and the Pacific, the government began to organize a broad-reaching effort to sustain patriotic fervor.

Urged on by the Office of War Information, the agency charged with overseeing the use of propaganda, Hollywood quickly began producing movies depicting the military aims. The government also recruited intellectuals to explain why the war needed to be fought and how citizens could help.

Artists, too, joined the campaign. The posters they created, often in response to government-sponsored contests, would prove to be some of the most enduring propaganda produced during the war. Displayed in government buildings and public spaces from coast to coast, their works helped galvanize support for the war with visceral visual power. In doing so, they employed a variety of persuasion strategies. While some encouraged people to contribute to the war effort by rationing or joining the workforce, other posters stoked fear of the enemy, sometimes using racist caricatures to breed hatred of Germany and Japan.

Though many were loath to get involved before Pearl Harbor, the country quickly rallied to provide both fiscal and moral support to the troops.

BUY THAT INVASION BOND!

Attention, Women!

JOIN THE WAAC
WOMEN'S ARMY AUXILIARY CORPS ★ U.S. ARMY

APPLY AT ANY U. S. ARMY RECRUITING AND INDUCTION STATION

Together We WIN

The military didn't just have its eyes on men—women were also courted for the war effort.

Pass the Ammunition

Produce for your Navy
VICTORY BEGINS AT HOME

SOLDIERS *without guns*

FOOD IS A WEAPON

DON'T WASTE IT !
BUY WISELY - COOK CAREFULLY - EAT IT ALL

FOLLOW THE NATIONAL WARTIME NUTRITION PROGRAM

Much of the material was designed to strike an emotional chord among citizens.

CHANGING TIMES

The military needed manpower, and posters aimed at recruitment for the armed services often underscored masculine strength with images of powerfully built men and mighty weaponry. Such posters, with their literal interpretation of American muscle, bolstered the nation's confidence and pride.

But men weren't the only ones to boost the war effort. As more young males joined the military, the U.S. faced acute labor shortages. Women were needed in factories turning out aircraft, ships and other weapons, and publicity campaigns urged them to get to work. In a drastic change from past generations, posters glorified the role of working women,

portraying them as attractive, confident and—above all—resolved to do their part to win the war. These posters suggested that femininity needn't be sacrificed while working at jobs traditionally done by men.

Racial segregation was part of American society during the war, and African Americans took part in the war effort with an eye toward breaking down racial barriers. (This objective was expressed by the "Double V" campaign launched in the nation's Black press, which called for victory over fascism abroad and victory over racism at home.) To combat racism, posters, pamphlets and films highlighted the participation and achievement of Blacks in military and civilian life.

Feeding and fueling America's growing war machine created shortages of gasoline, rubber, sugar, butter, meat and other goods on the home front. The government instituted a complex rationing system and put an enormous effort into explaining why it was necessary. Posters also encouraged civilians to conserve by joining car-sharing clubs, by saving waste kitchen fat for use in making explosives, and by participating in metal-collection drives. "Waste helps the enemy," noted one poster.

EMOTION AND REALISM

While some posters made use of symbolism or humor to drive home messages of patriotism and sacrifice,

THIS IS THE ENEMY

You TALK OF SACRIFICE...

HE *KNEW* THE MEANING OF SACRIFICE!

WINCHESTER

The posters could be graphic and disturbing, especially by mid-century standards.

the most effective posters, concluded the government, were those that presented realistic pictures in photographic detail in order to make a direct, emotional appeal. "War posters that are symbolic do not attract a great deal of attention, and they fail to arouse enthusiasm. Often, they are misunderstood by those who see them," noted a 1942 government guide for artists.

Many posters played on the public's fear of the enemy, with images of Americans living in imminent danger of German or Japanese domination. (A poster promoting war bonds, opposite page, showed children literally playing under the shadow of a Nazi swastika.) Some posters depicted atrocities that were committed in the name of fascism.

A prominent theme of the government's propaganda campaign was vigilance. Posters urged civilians to remember that enemy spies and saboteurs could well be lurking in their midst and warned them to avoid careless talk about troop movements and other information that could be used to help the enemy or undermine U.S. efforts.

THE MEANING OF SACRIFICE

Perhaps the most powerful messages were those concerning sacrifice. These went to the heart of the government's propaganda campaign by explaining in emotional terms why the country was at war and what it would cost to win. "The mortal realities of war must be impressed vividly on every citizen," noted a government manual for the motion picture industry, adding, "There is a lighter side to the war picture, particularly among Americans, who are irrepressibly cheerful and optimistic. But war means death. It means suffering and sorrow."

Posters depicting the grim reality of war—American soldiers lying dead on battlefields in far-off places—were meant to combat complacency that might be taking place at home. They reminded people that everyone would have to do their duty and stand guard before the war could end. ⊕

George Strock's 1942 picture of dead American soldiers at Buna Beach captured the reality of war.

DISPATCHES
FROM THE
FRONT

ERNIE PYLE AND OTHER WAR CORRESPONDENTS
TOLD AMERICANS WHAT THE FIGHTING IN EUROPE
AND THE PACIFIC LOOKED AND FELT LIKE.

Bill Mauldin, seen here in Italy in 1944, captured the life of ordinary American soldiers.

FOR PEOPLE AT home in the United States, newspapers, magazines and radio brought updates from the fighting on distant islands in the Pacific and remote villages in North Africa, Italy and France.

The news from far-flung correspondents and photographers was controlled by military censors, but the reality of war could not be kept hidden. Newspapers published lists of war dead, and in September 1943, almost two years after Pearl Harbor, Americans saw a photograph of dead American troops for the first time. That month, *Life* magazine published photojournalist George Strock's picture of three U.S. soldiers killed during the Battle of Buna-Gona in New Guinea, one of the many pivotal, if unsung, struggles in the Pacific. Taken on Dec. 31, 1942, the image was held up by U.S. Army censors for months while editors pushed to have it published.

President Franklin D. Roosevelt finally permitted the photo's release, hoping that it would inspire Americans to greater sacrifice. In an editorial, the magazine justified printing the image, noting that "words are never enough."

THE STORY OF GI JOE

Sometimes, though, the words could be entirely right. When American soldiers went to war, they were accompanied by a legion of bold war correspondents—reporters such as Homer Bigart of the *New York Herald Tribune*, who flew on bombing missions over Germany, and *Time* magazine correspondent William Walton, who parachuted into France prior to D-Day. They

Cartoonist Bill Mauldin created beloved soldiers "Willie and Joe" (right).

told American mothers and fathers not only how the war was going, but also how their sons were really faring overseas.

No reporter captured the story of GI Joe, the common U.S. soldier, better than Ernie Pyle, who wrote for the Scripps-Howard newspapers. To read Pyle's dispatches from the front was to see the war from the bottom up—not just as a procession of great military campaigns envisioned by generals, prime ministers and presidents, but as the dusty trail of "dogface" infantrymen advancing against America's enemies inch by soul-wearying inch.

In 1940 Pyle volunteered to cover the Battle of Britain, describing London to his readers as a city "ringed and stabbed by fire."

By 1942, Pyle was stationed with soldiers in North Africa. "At last we are in it up to our necks,

and everything is changed, even your outlook on life," he wrote. "Swinging first and swinging to kill is all that matters now."

THE DEATH OF CAPT. HENRY T. WASKOW

Pyle wrote about fighter pilots and Army engineers, covered the invasion of Sicily and described what it was like to be under fire in Italy. His most famous column, written on Jan. 10, 1944, from the front lines of the Italian campaign, lamented the death of a soldier, Capt. Henry T. Waskow of Belton, Texas. Waskow, noted Pyle, was beloved by his men. "He was very young, only in his middle twenties, but he carried in him a sincerity and gentleness that made people want to be guided by him," Pyle wrote.

He painted an intimate picture of the hard fighting in Italy: "Dead

men had been coming down the mountain all evening, lashed onto the backs of mules," wrote Pyle. "They came lying belly-down across the wooden pack-saddles, their heads hanging down on the left side of the mule, their stiffened legs sticking out awkwardly from the other side, bobbing up and down as the mule walked."

More bodies arrived throughout the night. "Four mules stood there, in the moonlight, in the road where the trail came down off the mountain," wrote Pyle, describing the scene. "The soldiers who led them stood there waiting. 'This one is Captain Waskow,' one of them said quietly."

The soldiers moved Waskow's body beside a low stone wall, noted Pyle. "The men in the road seemed reluctant to leave," he wrote. "They stood around, and gradually I could sense them moving, one by one, close to Captain Waskow's body. Not so much to look, I think, as to say something in finality to him and to themselves. I stood close by and I could hear."

"One soldier," wrote Pyle, "came and looked down, and he said out loud, 'God damn it!'"

BILL MAULDIN'S "WILLIE AND JOE"

If any journalist was as popular with the troops as Pyle, it was Bill Mauldin, a cartoonist for *Stars and Stripes,* the American soldiers' newspaper. He became famous for creating two archetypal infantrymen, Willie and Joe, who endured bad food, dirt and danger with sad-faced stoicism. In one poignant cartoon, the two are huddled in a marsh, their feet in the water. "Joe, yestiddy ya saved my life, and I swore I'd pay ya back," says Willie. "Here's my last pair of dry socks."

Officers sometimes didn't appreciate Mauldin's humor. When the cartoonist ridiculed Gen. George Patton's order that soldiers be clean-shaven at all times, even during combat, Patton called Mauldin an "unpatriotic anarchist" and threatened to throw him in jail and ban the *Stars and Stripes* from being read by his troops. Gen. Dwight Eisenhower stepped in and ordered Patton to back down.

One of Mauldin's most vocal fans, not surprisingly, was Ernie Pyle. "Mauldin's cartoons aren't about training-camp life, which you at home are best acquainted with," Pyle pointed out in one of his columns. "They are about the men in the line—the tiny percentage of our

Pyle's prose perfectly captured the heroism of the soldiers he met, but was neither sentimental nor maudlin.

vast army who are actually up there in that other world doing the dying. His cartoons are about the war."

"I'VE HAD IT"

In June 1944 Pyle was describing what he saw on the beaches of Normandy shortly after D-Day. "Now that it is over it seems to me a pure miracle that we ever took the beach at all," he reported. By that time, the toll on Pyle of bearing witness to the war's carnage was becoming apparent.

"It was a lovely day for strolling along the seashore," he wrote. "Men were sleeping on the sand, some of them sleeping forever. Men were floating in the water,

but they didn't know they were in the water, for they were dead."

Following D-Day, Pyle's dispatches often focused on the human cost of war. Once Paris was liberated, he wrote his final column from Europe. "I'm leaving," the weary correspondent told his readers. "'I've had it,' as they say in the Army."

Pyle returned back home to the U.S., but eventually he decided to cover the fighting still taking place in the Pacific. He accompanied Marines landing on Okinawa on April 1, 1945, and on April 18 Pyle was shot through the left temple by a Japanese machine-gunner. He died instantly. ✪

Ernie Pyle, seen here at work in Europe, died while reporting on the war in the Pacific.

VIRGINIA HALL

THE
SECRET WAR
AGAINST
THE NAZIS

HOW THE SPIES LEADING DANGEROUS
DOUBLE LIVES BEHIND ENEMY LINES
HELPED "SET EUROPE ABLAZE."

IN OCCUPIED FRANCE, Nazi-spy hunters played a tense cat-and-mouse game with local resistance fighters and the spies who helped them sabotage military targets and gather intelligence about German troop movements. Among the Allied agents operating in France, one was held in particular contempt by the Gestapo, the Nazi secret police.

Her name was Virginia Hall, and her story illustrates the daring of wartime spies working behind enemy lines. An American from a wealthy family, Hall was fluent in French, German and Italian, making her an ideal candidate for covert operations in Europe, first for a British spy agency called the Secret Operations Executive (SOE) and later for America's Office of Strategic Services (OSS), the precursor of the CIA.

While living in the French city of Lyon, Hall recruited a network of spies that included a bordello owner who passed along information his employees obtained from visiting German officers. Hall also masterminded a stunning prison escape to free captured Allied spies and also helped downed Allied aviators escape from France. And she did it all despite having a wooden leg.

The Nazis called her "the limping lady," and Klaus Barbie, the notorious Gestapo chief, vowed to get his hands on her. He never would.

OPERATION MINCEMEAT

Espionage played a crucial role in the war, and Europe became a web of spy rings and double agents. Winston Churchill created the SOE, in order to, as he put it,

Virginia Hall was presented with the Distinguished Service Cross in 1945—the only woman to receive the honor in WWII.

"set Europe ablaze" by planting bombs, gathering intelligence and supporting local resistance fighters. The rival British Secret Intelligence Service, or SIS, also gathered intelligence and ran elaborate deception operations.

Among the most famous British plots of World War II was Operation Mincemeat, which was designed to deceive the Nazis about the Allied invasion of Sicily in 1943. British intelligence obtained the body of a deceased derelict, dressed him as an officer of the Royal Marines and handcuffed him to a briefcase filled with false correspondence

"Virginia Hall, to a certain extent, was invisible. She was able to play on the chauvinism of the Gestapo at the time. None of the Germans... necessarily thought that a woman was capable of being a spy."

—CRAIG GRALLEY, FORMER CIA OFFICER

suggesting that the Allies planned to invade Greece and Sardinia.

Then they set the body adrift in the ocean off neutral Spain. When

In posters like this, Americans were warned of spies in their midst.

VIOLETTE SZABO

NANCY WAKE

it washed ashore, Spanish authorities delivered the fake documents to German spies, who were taken in by the ploy. Germany prepared to defend against an invasion in the wrong place.

THE SPYING GAME

Espionage professionals termed spying the "great game," but it was an incredibly dangerous one for anyone who was working under the noses of the enemy. New Zealand–born Nancy Wake lived a double life with her French husband in Marseilles, helping downed Allied airmen escape to Spain. As the Gestapo closed in on her in 1943, Wake managed to escape to Spain. Her husband, however, was captured

and executed. Wake then went to work for the SOE, parachuting back into France to work with French guerrilla fighters.

Another SOE agent, French-born Violette Szabo, parachuted into France in April 1944 to gather information, only to find that the spy ring she was working with had been exposed. She escaped to Britain and in June was sent to France once again. This time her luck ran out: Szabo was captured by the German army and later executed.

U-BOATS OFF LONG ISLAND

Not all the action was overseas. On the night of June 12, 1942, a German U-boat deposited a team of saboteurs on a beach near the

eastern tip of Long Island, New York. Discovered by a Coast Guard seaman patrolling the area, the head of the saboteurs, a man named George Dasch, tried to bribe the seaman, who later reported the incident, setting off a manhunt.

The Germans made their way to a hotel in Manhattan, but Dasch and another member of the team soon betrayed their comrades to the FBI; perhaps that was their intention all along, or perhaps they felt their cover had been blown. In the end, a military tribunal found the conspirators guilty of spying and condemned them to death. President Franklin D. Roosevelt commuted the sentence of the two saboteurs who'd exposed the plot, sending them to prison. The six others died by electrocution.

SPY QUEENS

An ideal recruit for the American OSS was once described as "a PhD who can win a bar fight," though in fact the OSS staff came from diverse backgrounds. From 1942 to 1945 the organization employed 13,000 people, a third of them women. Some broke codes, some produced propaganda and some, like Hall, operated from the shadows.

Before the war, Hall wanted to work for the U.S. Foreign Service but was rejected because she was a woman. She instead took a job as a clerk in the U.S. embassy in Warsaw, Poland, and later at the consulate in Turkey. There, while on a hunting expedition in 1933, Hall stumbled and shot herself in the foot. Her leg was amputated below the knee and she was fitted with a wooden appendage, which she promptly nicknamed "Cuthbert."

By 1940 Hall was living as a civilian in Paris. She drove ambulances for the French army during the Nazi invasion, then fled to London, where she was recruited by the British SOE.

AGENT IN PLACE

In 1941, Hall became the SOE's first long-term female resident agent in France. Posing as an American reporter with the *New York Post*, she was able to gather information and send news stories to her editor in New York that were embedded with coded reports for her SOE controllers in London.

Basing herself in Lyon, Hall dressed inconspicuously and often

JULIA CHILD

changed her appearance with makeup and disguises. In late 1942, with the Gestapo after her, Hall fled to the South of France, where she met a guide who led her to Spain on foot via a 7,500-foot pass in the Pyrenees mountains. There, Hall sent word to London that she was safe, adding, however, that Cuthbert was giving her trouble. Her controllers mistook Cuthbert for an informant and advised her to "have him eliminated."

When the SOE declined to send Hall on any more missions, she joined the American OSS instead and in 1944 returned to France.

There, she disguised herself as an aged peasant and organized a number of sabotage missions prior to D-Day. After the war, Hall became the only woman in World War II to receive America's Distinguished Service Cross. She continued working for the CIA until her retirement at age 60.

CELEBRITY SPIES

A number of well-known public personalities were also somewhat surprisingly involved in the great game of espionage during the war, including some of the following prominent figures:

JOSEPHINE BAKER The entertainer found stardom when she moved from New York to Paris in 1925. After the fall of France in 1940, she began aiding the French resistance by housing fugitives in her chateau in the south of France. She also gathered information about German troop movements by mingling with Nazis at chic soirees. smuggling the information out by recording it in invisible ink on sheet music.

MORRIS "MOE" BERG

MORRIS "MOE" BERG A professional baseball player for the Brooklyn Dodgers, Chicago White Sox, Cleveland Indians, Washington Senators and Boston Red Sox, Berg also studied modern languages at Princeton University and earned a law degree from Columbia University. As an OSS agent in Europe during the war, he helped gather information about the Nazis' attempt to build an atomic bomb.

JULIA CHILD When World War II broke out, the future TV chef joined the OSS, where she worked as a researcher. Later, as part of the OSS Emergency Sea Rescue Equipment Section, she helped cook up shark repellent. In 1944 and 1945 she was stationed in Ceylon (now Sri Lanka) and China.

IAN FLEMING The creator of secret agent James Bond left a dull life in banking to become the personal assistant to the head of British Naval Intelligence during World War II. He was later charged with creating and maintaining an intelligence network in Spain, an effort called Operation Goldeneye that also involved engineering sabotage missions against the Nazis. Fleming would later name his home in Jamaica "Goldeneye," and it was there that he wrote his famous espionage thrillers.

GRAHAM GREENE Recruited by Britain's MI6 and posted to Sierra Leone during World War II, the novelist was in charge of preventing the smuggling of resources from Africa into Germany. ⊕

JOSEPHINE BAKER

IAN FLEMING

GRAHAM GREENE

John Garfield (left) and Cary Grant crew a U.S. submarine in the 1943 movie *Destination Tokyo.*

HOLLYWOOD TAKES UP THE CAUSE

WITH AMERICA ON THE MARCH, TINSELTOWN
TURNED OUT A NEW KIND OF WEAPON: MOTION
PICTURES THAT BOOSTED MORALE AT HOME.

JUST MONTHS BEFORE America went to war, Humphrey Bogart became an A-list Hollywood movie star. After a decade of playing gangsters in genre films pumped out by Warner Bros., he starred as detective Sam Spade in *The Maltese Falcon*, which was released in October 1941 to wide critical and popular acclaim. The studio capitalized on the movie's success by quickly reuniting the film's cast, along with its director, John Huston, to make a movie called *Across the Pacific*.

Based on serialized magazine stories published earlier in 1941, the film's plot, as originally written, had Bogart's character averting a Japanese invasion of Pearl Harbor. But as production was gearing up, Japan really did attack the Hawaiian naval base. The project was shut down for three months, resuming production in March 1942 with a new script in which Bogart stops an attack on the Panama Canal.

Then, during filming, Huston was called up by the Army to make wartime documentaries. Completed by another director, *Across the Pacific* was finally in theaters in September 1942. In the meantime, Bogart had wrapped up filming another film project. It was a movie called *Casablanca*.

> **"The motion picture should be the best medium for bringing to life the democratic ideal.... The American people, on the whole, are not susceptible to The Strategy of Lies."**
> —U.S. OFFICE OF WAR INFORMATION

Released in January 1943 but set before the United States actually entered World War II, *Casablanca* told a story of romance and self-sacrifice, with Bogart's character, nightclub owner Rick Blaine, shedding his emotional isolation ("I stick my neck out for nobody," he says) as he embraces the fight against Nazi tyranny.

His evolution reflected isolationist America's changing attitudes toward the conflict and Hollywood's own changing role as America marched to war. By the time *Casablanca*

premiered, the American film industry had become a key part of the war effort. Army Chief of Staff Gen. George Marshall would later say that the war had seen the development of two new weapons— the airplane and the motion picture.

"THIS IS A BIG STORY"

Hollywood began turning out a few movies with war-related plots soon after Adolf Hitler's invasion of Poland in 1939. More appeared in 1940, after the invasion of France and the Battle of Britain, including *Foreign*

The evolution of Humphrey Bogart's character in *Casablanca* mirrored isolationist America's changing attitude toward the war.

"Ilsa, I'm no good at being noble, but it doesn't take much to see that the problems of three little people don't amount to a hill of beans in this crazy world."

—HUMPHREY BOGART, *CASABLANCA*

Correspondent, from British-born director Alfred Hitchcock. The cloak-and-dagger thriller ends with a journalist, played by Joel McCrea, describing the London Blitz to listeners in the United States during a radio broadcast.

"This is a big story and you're part of it," he says as German bombs thunder. "It's too late to do anything here now, except stand in the dark and let them come. It's as if the lights were all out everywhere, except in America. Keep those lights burning. Cover them with steel! Ring them with guns! Build a canopy of battleships and bombing planes around them! Hello, America! Hang on to your lights. They're the only lights left in the world."

Such calls for action infuriated American politicians who wanted to keep the U.S. out of the European war. In September 1942—the same month *Across the Pacific* was released—a United States Senate subcommittee began investigating whether Hollywood was campaigning to bring the United States into World War II by including pro-British messages in its films. The committee's head, isolationist Sen. Gerald Nye, said Hollywood was attempting to "drug the reason of the American people, set aflame their emotions, turn their hatred into a blaze, fill them with fear that Hitler will come over here and capture them."

As some historians have noted, however, Hollywood actually reacted relatively slowly to Hitler's threat, in part because studios were afraid of offending audiences in important European markets.

PROPAGANDA OR DEMOCRATIC IDEAL?

Hitler loved Hollywood films— Mickey Mouse and Greta Garbo were reportedly two of his favorite stars—and his propaganda chief, Joseph Goebbels, used the German film industry to court the masses.

While the United States government also recognized the power of cinema as propaganda, it wasn't as easy to co-opt the privately owned American film industry. The needs of the war effort had to

> **"The easiest way to inject a propaganda idea into most people's minds is to let it go through the medium of an entertainment picture."**
>
> —ELMER DAVIS,
> OFFICE OF WAR INFORMATION

be balanced against democratic values of free speech. President Franklin D. Roosevelt declared that there should be "no censorship" of movies, even as the government's Office of War Information (OWI) was put in charge of supervising Hollywood. The OWI supervised scripts to determine how they depicted America's war aims and America's enemies. Early on in the conflict, Hollywood chafed at the government's oversight, but by

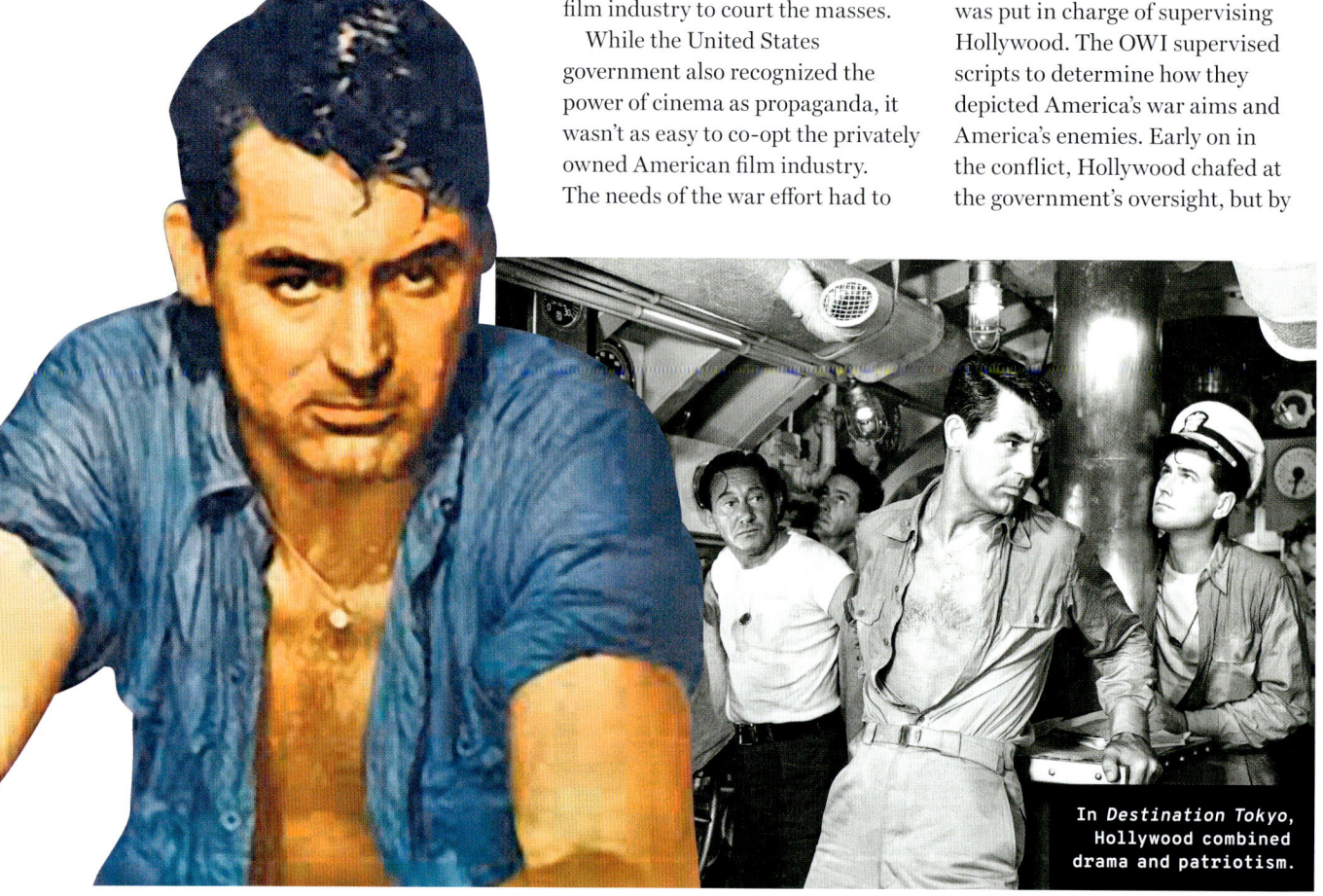

In *Destination Tokyo*, Hollywood combined drama and patriotism.

Cary Grant addresses his solemn crew in *Destination Tokyo*.

1943 filmmakers had learned that patriotism and profits could go hand in hand, as could censorship and sophisticated storytelling.

"MORE ROLLER SKATES IN THIS WORLD"

In 1943 Cary Grant starred as a U.S. Navy submarine commander in *Destination Tokyo*, a film that epitomized Hollywood's ability to combine emotional narrative and visual realism with messages the government wanted people to hear.

In one of the movie's more impassioned scenes, Grant addresses his men as they grieve over the death of a crewmate. Explaining the differences between American and Japanese society, he tells them that in Japan boys are presented with daggers at age 5 as part of a culture that breeds warriors, while American boys get roller skates. His point is clear: America, a land of peaceful people forced into war, was fighting to put an end to a bloodthirsty system run amok. "That's what Mike died for—more roller skates in this world—and even some for the next generation of Japanese kids," Grant says.

Donald Duck learned about life in Nazi Germany in the Walt Disney animated short *Der Fuehrer's Face*.

Hollywood's wartime films hit a variety of emotional notes about sacrifice and patriotism. Released in 1944, *The Sullivans* told the true story of five brothers who died serving aboard the same U.S. Navy ship. (The story would later inspire Steven Spielberg's 1998 film *Saving Private Ryan*.) Director John Ford's 1945 classic *They Were Expendable* was based on a bestselling book about U.S. Navy forces fighting against the odds during Japan's invasion of the Philippines.

DONALD DUCK AND HITLER

Hollywood also kept Americans laughing through the war. The comedy duo Abbott and Costello became popular in films like 1941's zany *Buck Privates*. Director Preston Sturges' 1944 comedy *Hail the Conquering Hero* was a warmhearted look at the plight of a man rejected by the Marines for health reasons.

American moviegoers ate up the Hollywood-made newsreels about the war, along with war-themed cartoons, perhaps most famously a 1943 Walt Disney short called *Der Fuehrer's Face*, in which Donald Duck toils in a nightmarish Nazi factory.

Somehow the studios managed to roll out the productions in spite of shortages of needed materials—including film stars who went off to serve in the military. Among them were James Stewart, who enlisted in the Army Air Corps in 1941, and Clark Gable, who enlisted in the Army Air Corps after his wife, the actress Carole Lombard, died in a 1942 plane crash while returning from a war-bond rally in Indiana.

Henry Fonda enlisted in the Navy, while Tyrone Power enlisted in the Marines.

"LOCKHEED—THATAWAY"

Like John Huston, directors John Ford, William Wyler, Frank Capra and George Stevens created documentary films for the military aimed at showing Americans not only what the war looked like, but why it needed to be fought. According to one estimate, by the war's end, one-quarter of men employed by Hollywood studios were in uniform.

Film studios improvised after the government's War Production Board issued an order setting limits on how much could be spent to create sets. The studios built sandbag air-raid shelters, while the use of searchlights was prohibited at movie

Donna Reed costarred with Robert Montgomery and John Wayne in *They Were Expendable*, which told a story of sacrifice.

Montgomery and Wayne defend the Philippines in *They Were Expendable*.

Fredric March starred in *The Best Years of Our Lives* in 1946.

Abbott and Costello starred in *Buck Privates*.

GOOD VERSUS EVIL

Hollywood's depiction of the war echoed the changes taking place in America through the war years. Before Pearl Harbor, war-themed movies often focused on the fanciful—stories about spies and GI hijinks. By 1943, films looked a lot more solemn and offered a realistic view of the fighting.

After the war, movies continued to reflect a changing world. In 1946, director William Wyler released *The Best Years of Our Lives*, an Oscar-winning movie about three former soldiers adjusting to civilian life. In 1949 audiences went to see both *Battleground*, a gritty film about the Battle of the Bulge, and *Twelve O'Clock High*, which depicted the psychological strain felt by aviators flying missions over Germany.

In 1955 came *The Dam Busters*, a British film about a famous World War II air raid that would later be an inspiration for director George Lucas' *Star Wars*. In 1962 Hollywood turned out *The Longest Day*, an all-star epic about the D-Day invasion. In 1981 the German film *Das Boot*—about life aboard a U-boat—won international recognition. In more recent years audiences have flocked to see movies like Steven Spielberg's *Schindler's List*, Clint Eastwood's *Letters From Iwo Jima* and Christopher Nolan's *Dunkirk*.

In the cinema, World War II has never ended. Audiences continue to be fascinated by this pivotal moment in history—a time of upheaval and battle that gave us the world we now live in. The war was also the quintessential story of good versus evil, and that's the kind of tale the movies have always loved to tell. ⊕

premieres to foil enemy bombing attacks. There was also worry that bombers might mistake the large studio facilities for nearby aircraft-manufacturing plants. Warner Bros. painted a big arrow on the top of a building with a sign reading, "LOCKHEED—THATAWAY."

Actors and actresses who didn't serve in the military helped to promote war bonds and entertain troops at home and abroad. In 1942, movie stars Bette Davis and John Garfield launched the Hollywood Canteen, a nightclub for servicemen on their way overseas. Stars such as Marlene Dietrich, Rita Hayworth and Hedy Lamarr waited on tables, while World War II pinup queen Betty Grable danced with soldiers. In 1944 Warner Bros. turned the real-life nightclub into the setting for a musical comedy film called *Hollywood Canteen*.

James Stewart and Clark Gable both enlisted in the Army Air Corps.

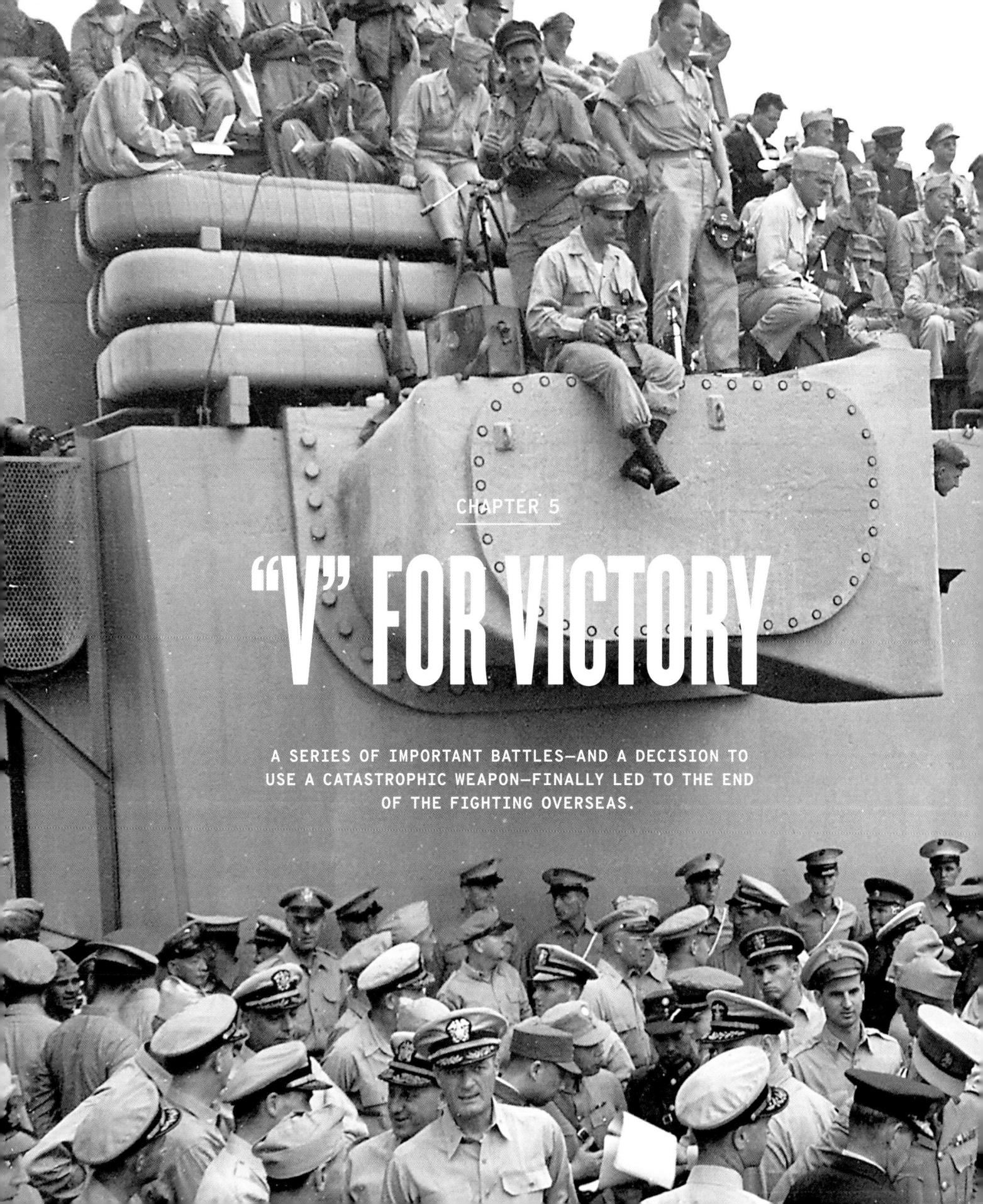

CHAPTER 5

"V" FOR VICTORY

A SERIES OF IMPORTANT BATTLES—AND A DECISION TO
USE A CATASTROPHIC WEAPON—FINALLY LED TO THE END
OF THE FIGHTING OVERSEAS.

0.016 SEC.
N

100 METERS

0.025 SEC.
N

100 METERS

0.090 SEC.
N

100 METERS

2.0 SEC.
N

100 METERS

Images of the Trinity test, the first detonation of a nuclear weapon, which took place on July 16, 1945.

END
GAME

AS ADOLF HITLER'S THIRD REICH
COLLAPSED, THE U.S. BROUGHT THE
CONFLICT IN THE PACIFIC TO A CLOSE
WITH A TERRIBLE NEW WEAPON.

THE BATTLE OF SAIPAN in June 1944 was emblematic of the fierce fighting in the Pacific and the appalling conditions in which Allied attackers and Japanese defenders lived and died.

In his book *War Letters*, a collection of missives written by soldiers in American wars, editor Andrew Carroll includes a note from Pvt. Richard King describing to his parents how men were "going crazy" in the South Pacific heat. "I couldn't open my mouth at all, my tongue was swollen five times its normal size, my throat burned to a crisp, and blood coming out of my nose and mouth," King wrote home.

In the book *Japan at War: An Oral History*, one of the few surviving Japanese soldiers on Saipan recalled living through the hellish Allied bombardment of the island. "We just clung to the earth in our shallow trenches," remembered Sgt. Takeo Yamauchi. "We were half buried. Soil filled my mouth many times. Blinded me. The fumes and flying dirt almost choked you."

Cut off from any hope of evacuation and preyed upon by U.S. Navy Hellcat fighter planes, Japanese troops hid in caves and wandered through a landscape littered with the bodies of their fallen comrades.

> **"The enemy has begun to employ a new and most cruel bomb, the power of which to do damage is, indeed, incalculable, taking the toll of many innocent lives."**
>
> —JAPANESE EMPEROR HIROHITO

Americans attack a German position at the Battle of the Bulge.

In the end, their commander, Gen. Yoshitsugu Saito, issued a final order, calling for a suicidal banzai charge into American guns.

Seven months later, Marines would fight for another island in the Pacific—a sulfuric spot of land just 750 miles off the Japanese coast named Iwo Jima. The battle there, against an enemy unwilling to surrender, would be among the bloodiest of the war.

HITLER'S DESPERATE MOVE

As Saipan was being secured in July 1944, U.S., British and Canadian armies were breaking out of Normandy and beginning their advance through France. That same month, a group of German military conspirators mounted a failed plot to assassinate Adolf Hitler and stage a coup d'état. By mid-August Paris had been liberated. By autumn, most of France, Belgium and part of the Netherlands had been liberated.

Hitler had greeted the Allied invasion of France with optimism. "The news couldn't be better," he boasted after D-Day. "As long as they were in Britain, we couldn't get at them. Now we have them where we can destroy them."

Against the advice of his senior military commanders, Hitler

Allied leaders gathered at the Yalta Conference in February of 1945.

devised a massive counterattack on the western front. It would come through the Ardennes—the same forested area in Belgium from which Germany had pounced on British and French armies in 1940.

THE BATTLE OF THE BULGE

With their supply lines stretched and their troops fatigued, the Allied armies had paused to regroup, assuming that the German military was all but finished. Instead, on Dec. 16, 1944, some 30 German divisions attacked American troops across an 85-mile front, distorting the Allied line and giving the battle its name. Fog grounded Allied aircraft, while historic cold added to the misery of American troops.

"NUTS!"

The Germans drove through undermanned American positions in the region. At a rugged area of the American line known as Schnee

> **"For the Germans the bulge is a springboard for any new blow; for the Americans it is too tempting a battleground to stay quiet. And the Americans, with the indomitable General Patton in the lead, are making the most of it."**
>
> —*THE NEW YORK TIMES*, JAN. 4, 1945

British soldiers cheered the news of Hitler's death in April 1945.

INSIDE HITLER'S BUNKER
THE FÜHRER'S FINAL DAYS

Adolf Hitler spent the last 105 days of his life underground. On Jan. 16, 1945, as Soviet armies began closing in on Berlin, Germany's leader descended into his Führerbunker, a 3,000-square-foot air-raid shelter constructed near the Reich Chancellery.

With him in this subterranean world were his mistress, Eva Braun, along with Nazi propaganda minister Joseph Goebbels and his family. Hitler kept to his usual patterns of living and working throughout the night and sleeping into the afternoon. He continued issuing orders to his military leaders whose armies had already been defeated.

Early on April 29, a local registrar was brought into the bunker to preside as Hitler and Braun married. There followed a gloomy breakfast at which the führer talked of happier times.

Hitler then called in his secretary to dictate his last will and testament. The document was filled with self-serving falsehoods and anti-Semitic ravings, placing the blame for the war on "international Jewry."

On the afternoon of April 30, Hitler, 56, and Braun, 33, retired to his study in the bunker. Their bodies were discovered together on a couch, his with a bullet hole in the right temple and Braun's smelling of cyanide.

In accordance with Hitler's will, Goebbels became German chancellor. The following day Goebbels and his wife died by suicide, after poisoning their six children with cyanide.

"**We the undersigned, acting by authority of the German High Command, hereby surrender unconditionally to the Supreme Commander, Allied Expeditionary Force and simultaneously to the Soviet High Command...**"

—DOCUMENT OF GERMAN SURRENDER

Photographer Joe Rosenthal's image showed a second, larger flag being raised over Iwo Jima.

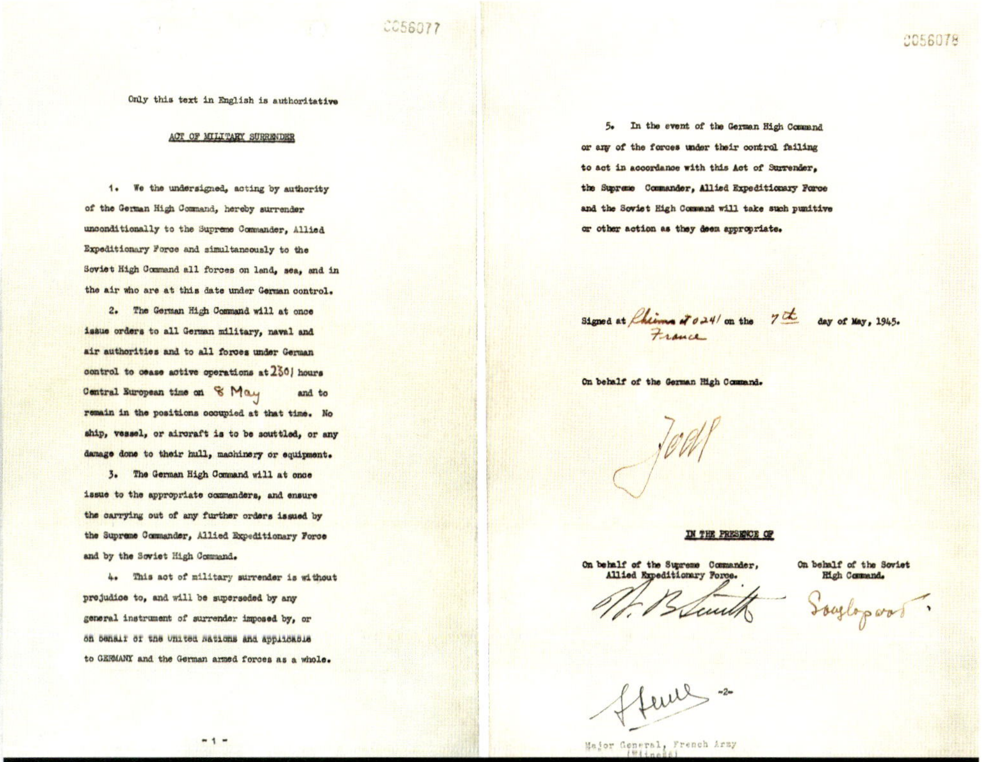

The "Act of Military Surrender" was signed by German Gen. Alfred Jodl.

Eifel, more than 6,000 U.S. troops were cut off and forced to surrender. Near the town of Malmedy, a group of American troops surrendered, and 84 were executed by Nazi SS troops. In the town of Bastogne, Germans surrounded 101st Airborne Division troops and demanded they surrender. Gen. Anthony McAuliffe replied with a one-word response that has since become legendary: "Nuts!"

By Christmas Eve, the worst of the attack was over, and as skies cleared Allied air power began to pound the Germans. Gen. George Patton moved his Third Army to Bastogne and readied to attack the Germans there. By mid-January the German army was back to where it had started, having suffered more than 100,000 casualties. Some 19,000 Americans were killed and 48,000 wounded in what was the largest and bloodiest single battle fought by the United States in World War II.

THE YALTA CONFERENCE

In early February, President Franklin D. Roosevelt met with British Prime Minister Winston Churchill and Soviet leader Joseph Stalin at the Yalta Conference in Soviet Crimea to discuss the shape of postwar Europe. By then Allied armies in the west were approaching the German

A week after Hitler's suicide, Germany's Gen. Alfred Jodl unconditionally surrenders and formally brings the war in Europe to a close on May 7, 1945.

border, while on the eastern front Soviet troops had driven back the Germans in Poland, Bulgaria and Romania and were within 40 miles of Berlin. At the conference, Stalin promised to allow free elections in Poland, though it would later become clear that the Soviet army had no intention of leaving conquered territories in eastern Europe.

THE BATTLE OF IWO JIMA

Eight days after the Yalta Conference ended, Marines landed on Iwo Jima. American military planners had assumed the fighting would be relatively easy, but the Marines learned otherwise when they hit the beaches. Lt. Col. Justus

M. "Jumpin' Joe" Chambers noted later that his battalion encountered interlocking bands of defensive firepower unlike anything he had faced on Saipan. "You could've held up a cigarette and lit it on the stuff going by," he recalled. "I knew immediately we were in for one hell of a time."

In command of the island's 21,000 Japanese troops was Gen. Tadamichi Kuribayashi, who decided to defend the island from positions hidden in Iwo Jima's mountains and dense jungles. America's overwhelming advantages in manpower, firepower and airpower ensured its ultimate victory, but the cost was terrible. More than 6,000 American troops were killed and 15,000 wounded during

the five-week battle, the greatest number of U.S. casualties in a single engagement of the Pacific war to date. All but 200 of the Japanese troops garrisoned on Iwo Jima died.

ICON OF WAR

On the fifth day of the battle, the Marines captured Mount Suribachi, the highest point on Iwo Jima. An American flag was raised at the summit, but a commander called for a bigger one that could be seen by troops below. Associated Press photographer Joe Rosenthal was on hand to document the second flag raising, creating what would become one of the best-known images of World War II.

Three of the six Marines originally identified as being in the photograph—Sgt. Michael Strank, Cpl. Harlon Block and Pvt. Franklin Sousley—were killed in action days after the flag raising. Pvt. Ira Hayes, Pfc. Rene Gagnon and Navy corpsman John Bradley went home to the U.S. as heroes to sell war bonds. In 1947, the military determined that Marine Sgt. Henry Hansen was one of the flag raisers, not Block. Hansen was also killed during the battle.

In 2016, it was determined that Marine Cpl. Harold Schultz, not Bradley, was shown in the photograph. And in 2019 historians determined that Marine Cpl. Harold Keller was in the photo rather than Gagnon.

OKINAWA: THE PRICE OF VICTORY

In Washington, D.C., Roosevelt could take solace in the victory at Iwo Jima. But as historian Doris Kearns Goodwin notes in her book *No Ordinary Time*, "the specter of Japanese zeal made it clear that the war in the Pacific would be even longer and bloodier than anyone had projected." As reports of the Iwo Jima fighting reached Washington, Secretary of War Henry Stimson met with Roosevelt to discuss America's atom bomb project.

The determination of Japanese troops became even clearer when, on April 1, more than 180,000 U.S. Army and Marine troops invaded the Pacific island of Okinawa. There they faced some 130,000 Japanese troops commanded by Gen. Mitsuru Ushijima. By June 22, 1945, the Americans had secured the island at a cost of 49,000 casualties, including 12,520 killed. Some 110,000 Japanese soldiers died. Among them was Ushijima, who committed ritual suicide.

BERLIN: THE RING CLOSES

In late March, Roosevelt took a train from Washington, D.C., to his retreat in Warm Springs, Georgia, hoping to regain his health. By all accounts his spirits were high, but on April 12, while talking with friends, he passed his right hand over his forehead several times, complained of "a terrific pain" in the back of his head and then collapsed, having suffered a massive cerebral hemorrhage. With his death, Vice President Harry S. Truman became the new leader of the United States.

In Europe, the end of Nazi Germany was near as Allied armies closed the ring around Hitler. On April 16, Soviet troops attacked Berlin from the east and south. On April 20, Hitler's birthday, the Soviets began shelling Berlin. In his Führerbunker, Hitler refused to admit defeat, but on April 30, as Soviet troops took control of the city, he died by suicide. (See "Inside Hitler's Bunker," page 163.) On May 7, Gen. Alfred Jodl, representing the German High Command, signed a document unconditionally surrendering all German military forces. The war in Europe was over.

THE TRINITY TEST

At 5:30 a.m. on July 16, 1945, scientists of the Manhattan Project detonated a plutonium bomb set atop a steel tower in the desert of New Mexico some 120 miles south of

> **"Having found the bomb we have used it.… It is an awful responsibility which has come to us. We thank God that it has come to us, instead of to our enemies; and we pray that He may guide us to use it in His ways and for His purposes."**
>
> —PRESIDENT HARRY TRUMAN

Albuquerque. Code-named Trinity, the first test of an atomic weapon produced an intense wave of light and heat and thunderous sound as a mushroom-shaped cloud rose 40,000 feet into the sky. The bomb exploded with a power equivalent to around 21,000 tons of TNT.

The decision to use the new weapon against Japan fell to Truman, who learned of the top-secret Manhattan Project only after becoming president in April.

How the decision was made, and why, has been the subject of debate ever since 1945. Some historians have held that using the bomb was unnecessary because Japan was already a defeated nation. Others have pointed to evidence that Japan may have been more open to surrendering than once thought. Some have argued that the bomb was used in part to establish America's global dominance in the postwar world. A number of American military commanders favored continuing a campaign of firebombing Japanese cities that had already suffered

The plutonium bomb nicknamed "Fat Man" was dropped on Nagasaki on Aug. 9, 1945.

the loss of hundreds of thousands of Japanese lives—a single raid against Tokyo in March killed 80,000. Meanwhile, a planned invasion of Japan, code-named Operation Downfall, was expected to result in millions of American dead and wounded and perhaps 10 million Japanese casualties. Against such a background, the U.S. president and his advisers weighed their options.

In late July 1945, Truman and other Allied leaders meeting in Potsdam, Germany, issued a statement calling for Japan's unconditional surrender. The Potsdam Declaration threatened the country with "prompt and utter destruction" if it failed to lay down its arms. Japan quickly rejected the terms of the ultimatum.

"LITTLE BOY"
Early on Aug. 6, 1945, an Army Air Force B-29 Superfortress bomber took off from Tinian, one of the Mariana Islands captured by the U.S. in 1944, loaded with a 9,700-pound uranium-235 bomb

The nuclear age began when America destroyed two Japanese cities with atom bombs.

nicknamed "Little Boy." The plane, named the *Enola Gay* after the mother of its pilot, Col. Paul W. Tibbets Jr., was headed for the Japanese city of Hiroshima, a manufacturing center about 500 miles from Tokyo.

Six and a half hours later, Tibbets maneuvered the plane toward an aiming point, the Aioi Bridge in the center of the city. At 8:15 a.m. local time, the *Enola Gay* dropped the bomb from an altitude of 31,000 feet. Forty-three seconds later, at 1,890 feet above the ground, it exploded. "The giant purple mushroom, which the tail-gunner had described, had already risen to a height of 45,000 feet, 3 miles above our own altitude, and was still boiling upward like something terribly alive," Tibbets later recalled.

Estimates of the death toll have varied somewhat over the years, but they generally indicate that between 60,000 and 80,000 people—roughly a third of Hiroshima's population—were killed in the blast. Another 50,000 to 70,000 were injured. (For more on the *Enola Gay* and its mission, see page 170.)

"ENDURING THE UNENDURABLE"

But the devastation failed to produce the desired response from the Japanese government, and on Aug. 9, another B-29 dropped a plutonium bomb nicknamed "Fat Man" on Nagasaki. Though more powerful than the "Little Boy" uranium bomb, the destruction caused by "Fat Man" was contained by the landscape near Nagasaki. Some 35,000 to 40,000 people were killed and an estimated 60,000 were injured.

Even after the bombing of Nagasaki, there was no clear consensus within the Japanese government on accepting the terms of surrender set forth at Potsdam. Emperor Hirohito intervened, however, and after several days, during which Japan's war ministry attempted a coup d'état in order to stop the surrender, Hirohito spoke on the radio to tell his people that Japan must accept defeat. It was the first time many had heard the emperor's voice.

"The hardships and sufferings to which our nation is to be subjected hereafter will be certainly great," he said in his address. "However, it is according to the dictates of time and fate that we have resolved to pave the way for a grand peace for all the generations to come by enduring the unendurable and suffering what is not sufferable."

ENOLA
GAY

"I knew we did the right thing," pilot Paul W. Tibbets Jr. said in a 2002 interview.

NO S

THE
FLIGHT
OF THE
ENOLA GAY

IN THE EARLY HOURS OF AUG. 6, 1945,
A U.S. BOMBER LOADED WITH AN ATOMIC
BOMB BEGAN A SIX-HOUR FLIGHT
TO JAPAN. NO ONE ON BOARD WAS CERTAIN
HOW THE MISSION WOULD END.

THE BOEING B-29 Superfortress was designed to fly farther, faster, and higher than any other bomber of World War II. It could carry 5,000 pounds of bombs to a target 1,500 miles away while cruising at 220 miles per hour at altitudes of up to 30,000 feet. Its pressurized and heated fuselage meant that the plane's 11-person crew didn't have to wear oxygen masks and heavy, bulky clothing. The bombers began flying missions in the Pacific in late 1944; in March of 1945, 300 B-29s attacked Tokyo, killing more than 100,000 people in 24 hours.

Five months later, on Aug. 6, 1945, a single B-29 carrying one bomb would destroy the Japanese city of Hiroshima, killing between 60,000 and 80,000 people.

The plane's pilot, Col. Paul W. Tibbets Jr. had had his mother's name, "Enola Gay," painted on the B-29 just before the mission. At 2:45 a.m., the plane roared off a runway on Tinian, one of the Mariana Islands taken by U.S. troops in 1944. With a crew of 12 and a 5-ton uranium bomb aboard, the aircraft was 15,000 pounds overweight, but it climbed smoothly into the darkness, accompanied by two other B-29s—one to record data about the atomic blast and the other to photograph it.

No one was quite sure how the flight would end. Would the plane reach its target? Would the bomb work? On board the *Enola Gay*, Tibbets carried a lucky cigarette case in one of his pockets. In another there was a small box containing 12 cyanide capsules, in case his crew fell into enemy hands.

During the flight, the *Enola Gay*'s navigator, Capt. Theodore "Dutch" Van Kirk, busied himself plotting the 1,500-mile, six-hour flight from Tinian to Hiroshima. Meanwhile, weaponeer Capt. William S. Parsons of the U.S. Navy activated the bomb. (Parsons had witnessed four B-29s crash and burn at takeoff, and he feared what might occur if that happened to a plane with an armed atomic bomb aboard.) Thirty minutes before reaching the target, Parsons' assistant, 2nd Lt. Morris R. Jeppson, inserted arming plugs into the bomb.

A little after 8 a.m., Tibbets began his bomb run over the target. Bombardier Tom Ferebee aimed for the center of Hiroshima. At 8:15 a.m. local time, the *Enola Gay* released the bomb from an altitude of 31,000 feet. Radar operator Jacob Beser tracked it as it fell 43 seconds to its predetermined detonation height, approximately 2,000 feet over the city.

After the explosion, the plane lurched upward as Tibbets began an evasive maneuver. Staff Sgt. George R. "Bob" Caron took a photograph of the mushroom cloud over Hiroshima, and the *Enola Gay*'s co-pilot, Robert Lewis, wondered to himself, "My God, what have we done?" The plane flew on, landing back at Tinian 12 hours later. ⊕

Crew members receive a briefing shortly before they depart. The bomb destroyed a 5-mile radius of Hiroshima.

To complete its mission, the design of the B-29 bomber was modified for both speed and strength.

Members of the 509th squadron back in the Mariana Islands after dropping the atomic bomb.

Sunshine reportedly broke through overcast skies as Japan formally surrendered on Sept. 2, 1945.

A NEW WORLD

THE CRUCIBLE OF WAR SET MANKIND
ON A PATH TOWARD AN ELUSIVE PEACE.

Nazi chieftain
Hermann Goering
took the stand
at the Nuremberg
trials in 1946.

IT WAS JUST after 9 a.m., Tokyo time, on Sept. 2, 1945, when Japanese Foreign Minister Mamoru Shigemitsu, acting on behalf of the Japanese government, signed the document of surrender aboard the USS *Missouri*, formally ending World War II. Gen. Yoshijiro Umezu, the Japanese Imperial Army chief of staff during the war's final years, then signed on behalf of the Japanese armed forces, while his aides wept.

Gen. Douglas MacArthur followed. After adding his name to the document, he said, "It is my earnest hope and indeed the hope of all mankind that from this solemn occasion a better world shall emerge out of the blood and carnage of the past." The ceremony ended shortly thereafter. It had taken a mere 20 minutes to end a war that had convulsed the world for six years.

A new world, the better one MacArthur spoke of, beckoned on the horizon. The nationalistic fury that had driven the world to war was giving way to new multilateral institutions and monetary systems binding countries together.

In America, an economy that had been transformed by the energy of wartime production was set to usher in a new era of prosperity from which a mighty middle class would grow. In the wake of the atrocities of the Holocaust and military crimes against humanity, new declarations supporting the concept of human rights would be established.

And just as this was happening, the world plunged into a new kind of conflict. As the alliance between the victors of World War II frayed, a rift grew that would split Europe in two. With the dawn of the atomic age, the rupture would turn into a terrifying Cold War between the globe's two new superpowers, the United States and the Soviet Union.

THE COST OF WAR
Numbers are an insufficient means of expressing the nature of the

Margaret Bourke-White documented the liberation of Buchenwald.

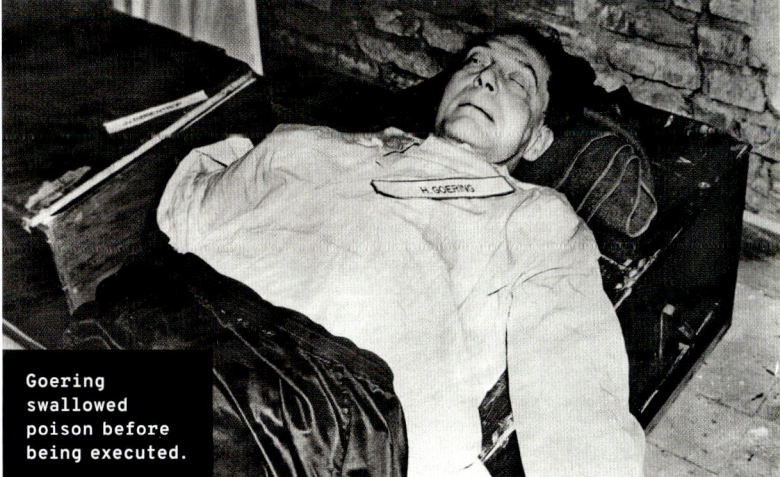

Goering swallowed poison before being executed.

catastrophe that was loosed on the world in the 1940s. That job properly belongs to storytellers—the historians, filmmakers and journalists who have investigated the war and continue in their attempts to explain its cruelty. Nonetheless, numbers are necessary to describe the scale of the war's misery.

Estimated death tolls from World War II vary widely, but many suggest that some 80 million people died in the war. That represents about 4% of the world's population in 1940. Most of the dead—up to 55 million by some estimates—were civilians. Millions more, civilian and military, were wounded. According to one estimate, at least 11 million and perhaps up to 20 million people were displaced by combat operations and ethnic cleansing during the war.

According to the National World War II Museum, the Soviet Union lost 24 million people, more than one-tenth of its population, with some 8 million killed in battle. Twenty million Chinese people died, many from starvation. The death toll for Germany was between 6.6 and 8.8 million, with 5.5 million killed in battle. Japan lost up to 3.1 million people, two-thirds of them in battle. The United Kingdom lost 450,700 people, with 383,600 killed in battle.

The United States got off lightly in comparison. Almost all of the 418,500 Americans killed in the war were in the military.

BARBARIC ACTS

Among the dead were at least 10 million killed during the Holocaust, 6 million of them Jews. As Allied armies liberated Nazi concentration camps in the spring of 1945, they encountered scenes that words could scarcely describe. "The things I saw beggar description," noted Gen. Dwight Eisenhower.

Life magazine photographer Margaret Bourke-White, who entered Germany with Gen. George Patton's Third Army, was among the first to document the reality of the

President Roosevelt and representatives of 26 United Nations allies gather in 1942.

atrocities. Her images of survivors at the Buchenwald concentration camp, taken in April 1945, remain among the most haunting of the war.

"I kept telling myself that I would believe the indescribably horrible sight in the courtyard before me only when I had a chance to look at my own photographs," Bourke-White later wrote. "Using the camera was almost a relief; it interposed a slight barrier between myself and the horror in front of me."

In 1945, the Allies established the International Military Tribunal in Nuremberg, Germany, to prosecute and punish war criminals, culminating in the landmark Nuremberg trials from November 1945 to October 1946. The trials ended with death sentences being handed down for 12 top Nazi officials. The executions were carried out on Oct. 16, 1946. Two hours before he was to be hanged, Hermann Goering, the Nazi chieftain who led Germany's Luftwaffe, killed himself by swallowing a vial of poison that had been smuggled into his cell.

In Tokyo, the International Military Tribunal for the Far East sentenced seven Japanese civilian and military officials to death for war crimes. Japan's wartime Prime Minister, Hideki Tojo, tried but failed to kill himself after his arrest was ordered in 1945. He was hanged on Dec. 23, 1948.

FDR'S DREAM: THE UNITED NATIONS

Soon after the United States entered the war in 1941, President Franklin D. Roosevelt coined a term for the alliance of countries

> **"Europe's requirements...of foreign food and other essential products... are so much greater than her present ability to pay that she must have substantial additional help."**
>
> —GEORGE C. MARSHALL, 1947

that had formed to fight the Axis Powers. He called them the "United Nations." This alliance would also become the basis for one of Roosevelt's most cherished dreams—an international institution that would maintain peace after the war ended. During the war, a number of meetings were held by the Allies to hammer out the framework for a postwar United Nations, and at the Yalta Conference in 1945 Roosevelt pushed to finalize an accord to establish the organization.

In his quest to create the United Nations, Roosevelt was guided by the example of another U.S. president, Woodrow Wilson, who had promoted a similar peacekeeping entity, the League of Nations, after World War I. The Senate rejected the League, however, shattering Wilson's presidency and setting the country on a path toward isolationism.

STALIN'S REALITY: A DIVIDED EUROPE

The League of Nations ultimately proved ineffective in keeping the peace, its ambitious aims undercut by a number of problems, including

This rare £1M bank note (left) was printed in connection with the Marshall Plan.

The European Recovery Plan, or Marshall Plan, was enacted in 1948.

a cumbersome structure that called for decisions to be made by unanimous vote. Plans for the United Nations—including veto power for the U.S., Britain, China and the Soviet Union—sidestepped many of its predecessor's flaws. Roosevelt returned from Yalta satisfied: Soviet dictator Joseph Stalin had approved the plans for the United Nations, and he had promised that all nations would have the right to choose their own postwar governments.

Those promises meant little, however, given the current situation in Europe. With Soviet troops and tanks occupying conquered lands in Eastern and Central Europe, the region had already fallen under Stalin's thumb. Roosevelt was quick to understand the reality of the geopolitical situation.

"I didn't say the result was good," the president told an aide after Yalta. "I said it was the best I could do."

On July 28, 1945, a little more than three months after Roosevelt's death, the Senate fulfilled his dream by ratifying the United Nations Charter, signaling an important change in America's involvement in world affairs. Meanwhile, Europe was already solidifying into Eastern and Western blocs.

WINNING THE PEACE: THE MARSHALL PLAN

The United States projected itself even further into global affairs in 1948 when it initiated the European Recovery Plan. The program was the brainchild of George C. Marshall, who had served as the U.S. Army chief of staff during the war and had gone on to become secretary of state under President Harry Truman. The Marshall Plan, as it came to be known, provided $12 billion—around $130 billion in today's money—to help rebuild the cities and economies of Western European nations.

Its goals weren't only humanitarian in nature. After World War I, weakened nations had lurched toward fascism; Marshall hoped his plan would stop the spread of Communism beyond the Soviet Union's sphere of influence in Eastern Europe. Fearing U.S. interference, the Soviet Union and its satellite countries, including Poland and Czechoslovakia, rejected any American help. Britain, France and West Germany were among the countries receiving most of the aid.

The effectiveness of the Marshall Plan in reviving postwar Europe has been debated by economists and historians in the subsequent decades since World War II ended, although it has won wide praise for helping ravaged countries and for its role in supporting democracies throughout Europe.

NUCLEAR BRINKSMANSHIP: THE COLD WAR

Politically, the Marshall Plan helped to cement the divisions between Eastern and Western Europe and served as a catalyst for the formation of a Western military alliance, the North Atlantic Treaty Organization, or NATO, in 1949. Some historians cite the Marshall Plan as the beginning of the Cold War, the decades-long global competition that defined geopolitics in the age of nuclear weapons.

The Soviet Union tested its first atomic bomb—called RDS-1 or "First Lightning" and code-named Joe-1 by the U.S.—in 1949. In 1952, the United States tested a far more powerful hydrogen bomb. The Soviets then tested their own hydrogen bomb a year later. The result of this escalating arms race was a "balance of terror" that emerged in the form of a concept called Mutually Assured Destruction, or MAD, which held that direct military engagement between the United States and the

The Soviet Union tests its first atomic bomb in 1949.

East Germany erects the Berlin Wall to partition the city in 1961.

The Berlin Wall ran 96 miles in length, 27 miles within Berlin. At least 327 people died trying to cross it.

Soviet Union would inevitably lead to a nuclear apocalypse.

Instead, the Cold War was fought through proxy wars—including the Korean War and the Vietnam War—and bids for ideological influence. By the late 1950s, the race to build ever more powerful missiles turned into a space race as the U.S. and the Soviet Union vied to put satellites and humans into orbit. The space race would eventually lead to America's Apollo missions to the moon.

The Cold War began to take shape soon after the fall of Nazi Germany, when the victorious Allies divided the country in two—part under the control of Western powers and part under the control of the Soviet Union. In addition, the city of Berlin, which lay inside the Soviet sector, was divided between East and West. In 1949 the Western Allies merged their sectors of the country, creating a new nation, the Federal Republic of Germany, or simply West Germany. The Soviet Union responded by creating the German Democratic Republic, or East Germany.

Berlin remained divided. Perhaps the most enduring symbol of the Cold War was a concrete wall built by East Germany in 1961 to partition the city. The wall, the scene of many real and fictional spy tales, finally came down in 1989, as the Soviet Union began to collapse. In 1990 East Germany and West Germany reunited, and the Cold War that had begun at the end of World War II came to an end.

AMERICA'S BOOM, AND BOOMERS

At the close of the Second World War the United States took its

> **"A shadow has fallen upon the scenes so lately lighted by the Allied victory.... From Stettin in the Baltic to Trieste in the Adriatic an iron curtain has descended.... Behind that line lie all the capitals of Central and Eastern Europe."**
>
> —WINSTON CHURCHILL, 1946

place as the most powerful and prosperous nation on Earth. With peace, industries that had been making airplanes and munitions began to turn out goods for consumers eager to spend money.

New car sales quadrupled between 1945 and 1955. The GI Bill, enacted to help give a boost to returning veterans, made low-interest mortgages available, spurring residential home construction. Real estate developer William J. Levitt used assembly-line techniques to pioneer the creation of suburban communities on a large scale.

With servicemen returning home, a different kind of boom took place. In 1946, 3.4 million babies were born, 20% more than in 1945. In 1947, another 3.8 million babies were born, and more than 4 million were born every year from 1954 until 1964. All those babies—today's "boomers"—would play an important role in shaping the culture, politics and economy of the United States.

American culture changed at almost every level. In 1948, brothers Richard and Maurice McDonald opened a drive-in restaurant in San Bernardino, California, to quickly

In 1948, two brothers named McDonald started feeding postwar Americans fast and cheap meals.

In 1946, the return of servicemen led to a huge baby boom in the U.S.

feed cheap meals to busy workers. Their innovations helped create the modern fast-food industry. In 1944, a Black Army lieutenant named Jackie Robinson faced a court martial after he refused to sit in the back of a military bus at Fort Hood, Texas. He was eventually acquitted, and in 1947 he broke Major League Baseball's color barrier when he began playing for the Brooklyn Dodgers. In doing so, he helped open a new chapter in American racial equality.

"THE HUMAN TRAGEDY"

In the preface to his six-volume memoir of the war, Winston Churchill lamented the world's failure to find a lasting accord. "The human tragedy," he wrote, "reaches its climax in the fact that

In 1947, Army veteran Jackie Robinson broke baseball's color barrier.

after all the exertions and sacrifices of hundreds of millions of people and of the victories of the Righteous Cause, we have still not found peace or security, and that we lie in the grip of even worse perils than those we have surmounted."

The world has certainly not found much peace in the years since the surrender of Germany and Japan in 1945. With the end of the Cold War, new conflicts and international crises have arisen, despite multilateral institutions like the World Bank (founded in 1944), the International Monetary Fund (founded in 1945) and the United Nations.

In 1948, the U.N. adopted the landmark Universal Declaration of Human Rights, which has been codified through international treaties and national constitutions. Yet human rights atrocities have persisted. Meanwhile, the nationalist sentiments that postwar leaders feared have grown in recent years, even as the calamity of the 1940s fades further into the past.

LOOKING BACK

Even today, we run the risk of reflecting upon the war with the

The GI Bill helped spur residential home construction.

complacent assumption that its outcome was inevitable. That is not how it felt to many people in 1940 and 1941. As some military historians have pointed out, if Hitler had launched his surprise attack on the Soviet Union a month earlier—in May of 1941, rather than June—his armies might have reached Moscow before the Russian winter stopped them. In that case, the history of the war might have looked far different.

We also look back at the war through the scrim of a modern culture that has sanitized and romanticized the fighting. That the war was terrible, that it was suffused with moral ambiguity, there can be no doubt. Ernie Pyle, the American journalist who saw so many battles, once wrote to his wife from the front line in Sicily, "The war gets so complicated and confused in my mind; on especially sad days it's almost impossible to believe that anything is worth such mass slaughter and misery."

There can also be no doubt, however, that there was nobility and necessity in the desperate fight against a darkness that threatened to engulf humanity. ⊕

CENTENNIAL BOOKS

An Imprint of
Centennial Media, LLC
40 Worth St., 10th Floor
New York, NY 10013, U.S.A.

CENTENNIAL BOOKS is a trademark of Centennial Media, LLC

ISBN 978-1-951274-70-2

Distributed by
Simon & Schuster, Inc.
1230 Avenue of the Americas
New York, NY 10020, U.S.A.

For information about custom editions, special sales and premium and corporate purchases,
please contact Centennial Media at contact@centennialmedia.com.

Manufactured in Singapore

10 9 8 7 6 5 4 3 2 1

Publishers & Co-Founders Ben Harris, Sebastian Raatz
Editorial Director Annabel Vered
Creative Director Jessica Power
Executive Editor Janet Giovanelli
Features Editor Alyssa Shaffer
Deputy Editors Ron Kelly, Anne Marie O'Connor
Managing Editor Lisa Chambers
Design Director Martin Elfers
Senior Art Director Pino Impastato
Art Directors Patrick Crowley, Natali Suasnavas, Joseph Ulatowski
Copy/Production Patty Carroll, Angela Taormina
Assistant Art Director Jaclyn Loney
Senior Photo Editor Jenny Veiga
Production Manager Paul Rodina
Production Assistant Alyssa Swiderski
Editorial Assistant Tiana Schippa
Sales & Marketing Jeremy Nurnberg